UNDERSTANDING
BERYL BAINBRIDGE

Understanding Contemporary British Literature
Matthew J. Bruccoli, Series Editor

Volumes on

Understanding Kingsley Amis • Merritt Moseley
Understanding Martin Amis • James Diedrick
Understanding Beryl Bainbridge • Brett Josef Grubisic
Understanding Julian Barnes • Merritt Moseley
Understanding Alan Bennett • Peter Wolfe
Understanding Anita Brookner • Cheryl Alexander Malcolm
Understanding John Fowles • Thomas C. Foster
Understanding Michael Frayn • Merritt Moseley
Understanding Graham Greene • R. H. Miller
Understanding Kazuo Ishiguro • Brian W. Shaffer
Understanding John le Carré • John L. Cobbs
Understanding Doris Lessing • Jean Pickering
Understanding Ian McEwan • David Malcolm
Understanding Iris Murdoch • Cheryl K. Bove
Understanding Tim Parks • Gillian Fenwick
Understanding Harold Pinter • Ronald Knowles
Understanding Anthony Powell • Nicholas Birns
Understanding Will Self • M. Hunter Hayes
Understanding Alan Sillitoe • Gillian Mary Hanson
Understanding Graham Swift • David Malcolm
Understanding Arnold Wesker • Robert Wilcher
Understanding Paul West • David W. Madden

UNDERSTANDING
BERYL
BAINBRIDGE

Brett Josef Grubisic

The University of South Carolina Press

© 2008 University of South Carolina

Published by the University of South Carolina Press
Columbia, South Carolina 29208

www.sc.edu/uscpress

Manufactured in the United States of America

17 16 15 14 13 12 11 10 09 08   10 9 8 7 6 5 4 3 2 1

Library of Congress Cataloging-in-Publication Data

Grubisic, Brett Josef.
    Understanding Beryl Bainbridge / Brett Josef Grubisic.
        p. cm. — (Understanding contemporary British literature)
    Includes bibliographical references and index.
    ISBN 978-1-57003-756-6 (cloth : alk. paper)
    1. Bainbridge, Beryl, 1933– —Criticism and interpretation. I. Title.
    PR6052.A3195Z68 2008
    823'.914—dc22

                                                            2008018596

Contents

Series Editor's Preface / vii

Chapter 1
Understanding Beryl Bainbridge / 1

Chapter 2
Opening Strategies
A Weekend with Claude, Another Part of the Wood,
and *Harriet Said* / 19

Chapter 3
Perilous Aspirations
The Dressmaker and *The Bottle Factory Outing* / 47

Chapter 4
Domestic Lives
Sweet William, A Quiet Life, and *Injury Time* / 74

Chapter 5
Closures and Transitions
Young Adolf, Winter Garden, Watson's Apology, and
An Awfully Big Adventure / 102

Chapter 6
Fictions of History
*The Birthday Boys, Every Man for Himself, Master
Georgie,* and *According to Queeney* / 133

Notes / 167
Bibliography / 181
Index / 189

Series Editor's Preface

The volumes of *Understanding Contemporary British Literature* have been planned as guides or companions for students as well as good nonacademic readers. The editor and publisher perceive a need for these volumes because much of the influential contemporary literature makes special demands. Uninitiated readers encounter difficulty in approaching works that depart from the traditional forms and techniques of prose and poetry. Literature relies on conventions, but the conventions keep evolving; new writers form their own conventions—which in time may become familiar. Put simply, *UCBL* provides instruction in how to read certain contemporary writers—identifying and explicating their material, themes, use of language, point of view, structures, symbolism, and responses to experience.

The word *understanding* in the titles was deliberately chosen. Many willing readers lack an adequate understanding of how contemporary literature works; that is, what the author is attempting to express and the means by which it is conveyed. Although the criticism and analysis in the series have been aimed at a level of general accessibility, these introductory volumes are meant to be applied in conjunction with the works they cover. They do not provide a substitute for the works and authors they introduce, but rather prepare the reader for more profitable literary experiences.

M. J. B.

CHAPTER 1

Understanding Beryl Bainbridge

> I was not an objective traveler. There are people who live in the present and those who live for the future. There are others who live in the past. It would seem we all have little choice. Early on, life dictates our preferences. All my parents' bright days had ended before I was born. They faced backwards. In doing so they created in me so strong a nostalgia for time gone that I have never been able to appreciate the present or look to the future.
>
> Beryl Bainbridge, *English Journey*

Books by Beryl Bainbridge have appeared regularly since her first novel, *A Weekend with Claud*, debuted in 1967. *According to Queeney*, her sixteenth novel, was published in 2001, and it stands as a testimonial to the author's long-standing engagement with fiction: Bainbridge wrote a novella titled *Filthy Lucre, or The Tragedy of Ernest Ledwhistle and Richard Soleway* between 1 June and 18 August 1946, at age eleven, and had written several macabre short stories the year before. She recalls believing "even then, that a short story was a waste of a good idea" and with apparent pragmatism eventually directed much of her writing practice toward the novel form.[1]

Bainbridge was born in Liverpool on 21 November 1934 and grew up about twelve miles from that city in Formby, a coastal town. She was educated at Merchant Taylors' School, from which she was expelled at age fourteen for writing a racy limerick. Her first occupation, in theater, began when she was sixteen, and she continued her professional involvement with it as late as 1972. That varied career, encouraged by her stage-managing mother, started with tap-dancing lessons at age six, ballet, and instruction at the Arts Educational Schools. She had performed on radio by age ten and had acted on stage by age fifteen. As captured in bittersweet detail in her autobiographical novel *An Awfully Big Adventure* and her travel memoir, *English Journey, or The Road to Milton Keynes*, employment in theater meant performing on stage as a "character juvenile" as well as being involved with technical matters behind the scenes as an assistant stage manager.[2]

In response to intensifying quarrels at home, Bainbridge ran off to London when she was fifteen. She soon returned home and found work in a Liverpool repertory company.[3] A year later she met and "fell hopelessly in love" with an artist named Austin Davies, a stage designer at the Playhouse Theatre, where Bainbridge was playing Ptolemy in Shaw's *Caesar and Cleopatra*.[4] The troubled romantic relationship, which she sought to complicate by running away once again to London and to discourage altogether by converting to Catholicism in Scotland, did nonetheless culminate in marriage in 1954. The two were divorced in 1959. Their children, Aaron Paul and Johanna Harriet (the father of her third child, Ruth Emmanuella, was Scottish novelist and screenwriter Alan Sharp), lived with their mother in Liverpool after the divorce; Bainbridge began to write *Harriet Said*, her first undertaking as a novelist, during her pregnancy with Aaron Paul. In the early 1960s the family moved to London because Davies wanted the children to live nearby. Though Bainbridge resides in London and has done so since her eventual reclusive settling in a Camden Town Victorian-era house in about 1970,[5] her affinity for Liverpool remains powerful. In *English Journey* she recalls, "I left Liverpool twenty years ago, and though I revisit it a dozen times a year, summer and winter, I can no longer claim to be a citizen. Yet I am so tied to it by the past, by memories of family and beginnings, that I still think of it as home."[6]

Not averse to autobiographical musings, Bainbridge has stated that her "terrifying" experiences in early life had a profound impact on her sensibility and craft:[7]

> All my childhood was spent with people who were disappointed. They'd married the wrong person, failed in employment, been manipulated by others. They took a fierce pride in knowing themselves for what they were. Not for them the rosy view of life, the helpful excuses that might explain and mitigate. They gave each other labels—fifth-columnist, skinflint, hysterical baggage, Wreck of the Hesperus. Class-conscious, they were either dead common or a cut above themselves. In the family album it was true there were some faded snapshots of holidays at Blackpool, everyone smiling and fooling on the sands, but it must have been a trick of the camera.[8]

Her unhappy parents, familial poverty, and wartime deprivation were formative, so much so that in interviews and essays published decades after her childhood Bainbridge consistently refers to her mature self as having been forged and fixed into place when she was a girl. The childhood of her recollections is dominated by discord. For example, in *English Journey* she recalls, "All my parents' bright days had ended before I was born. They faced backwards."[9] She often depicts her mother, Winifred, sympathetically—as caring and encouraging if under duress because of her "unfortunate experience of marriage."[10] Even so, she has also stated that her convention-bound mother was preoccupied with class distinctions and taught her daughter that men were creatures of privilege even though Winifred herself was superior to any man. Bainbridge has expressed both reservation and clear disdain for her manic father, Richard, a salesman. In *English Journey*, for instance, she speaks of her father as an unhappy man who was fond of telling stories about his illustrious past, the veracity of which she is unable to distinguish: "As he was a proud man and a failure according to his own lights I cannot be sure that what he told me was the truth."[11] She qualifies his stories (with statements such as "if he was to be believed") and frequently refers to their quarrels (for example, "Throughout my childhood, on the occasions when we were on speaking terms").[12] By firmly establishing her father's contradictory nature ("a flair for profit yet a committed socialist all his life") and his constant bluster ("my father was always raving about the Yellow Peril"), she asserts, in addition, the towering influence of his personality.[13] From her adult perspective, moreover, Bainbridge views the failure of her parents' dreams and fond affinity for their halcyon days with a certain fatalism: "In doing so they created in me so strong a nostalgia for time gone that I have never been able to appreciate the present or look to the future."[14]

Although she remembers herself as being a reserved and bookish girl greatly intrigued by the writings of D. H. Lawrence, Denton Welch, John Steinbeck, and Charles Dickens, Bainbridge also gives her unhappy childhood experiences a central place in the forging of her eventual career as a novelist. In "How I Began," a 1994 essay that prefaces *Collected Stories*, Bainbridge explains the genesis of her work as a defensive response to a dismaying family life: "My father and mother bickered a lot, which is why, there being no such thing as television to distract me, or any other room in which to escape from the raised voices, my mother encouraged my natural inclination to scribble in note-books."[15] In that same brief essay she recalls writing short sto-ries at age eight and *Filthy Lucre* at ten, and she views their purpose as being fundamentally therapeutic, stating that writing was "more beneficial an occupation to us than attending a psy-chiatric clinic, should such a place have existed, and helped get rid of anxieties nurtured by the particularly restricted sort of up-bringing common to lower-class girls in wartime England."[16]

Besides offering insight into her own perceptions about her development as a writer—an occupation that includes novels, short stories, nonfiction, television scripts, a weekly newspaper column for the *Evening Standard* (1986–92; published as *Some-thing Happened Yesterday*), and theater criticism for the maga-zine *Oldie* (1992–2002; published as *Front Row: Evenings at the Theatre*)—Bainbridge's autobiographical vignettes provide guidance to her novels' themes, affinities, and preoccupations. Even granting a direct correlation between Bainbridge's auto-biographical statements and her own output as a novelist, it might be beneficial to understand her comments as pointing toward developments in, rather than fully mapping or explicat-ing, her own work. Her comments are suggestive and, if nothing else, indicative of the manifold ways the artist's personal experi-ences have been transmuted into her art. Consider, for instance, the ambiguity of the comment about her parents' influence in *English Journey*: "In doing so they created in me so strong a nos-talgia for time gone that I have never been able to appreciate the present or look to the future."[17] Here one probable implica-tion is that Bainbridge's fiction would compulsively avoid the present and dwell in an idealized past. Until 1978's *Young Adolf*

Bainbridge's fiction was commonly set in or near the present day. Moreover, since the author's depictions of past eras—whether London circa 1853, Crimea in 1854, or Liverpool circa 1911—are anything but idyllic, it is clear that Bainbridge's real-life nostalgia does not animate or even necessarily color her fictional visions of the past.

Likewise, although she has a proclaimed inability to appreciate the present, it is less certain how that apparent jadedness or disaffection molds her depictions of the present. Certainly those representations, beginning with the hostile and generally unredeemable characters of *A Weekend with Claud*, tend to highlight the baser qualities of humanity; but to simply proclaim that Bainbridge's personal alienation from the present day and nostalgia for "time gone" results in antagonistic portrayals of the contemporary is both reductive (so that the author becomes nothing other than a conservative ideologue with an ax to grind) and void of illumination. Qualifying commentary aside, Bainbridge does identify personal experiences and traits that plainly relate to her fiction. In particular her references to the macabre, humor, disillusionment with the present, affinity for the past, and awareness of both the destructive and disabling role of culture and interpersonal relationships warrant further consideration because these qualities pervade her novels.

Well regarded in England but less well known in North America, Bainbridge has attracted widespread critical praise, which commonly takes note of her technical skills and eccentric vision. Frank Kermode, for instance, describes her as "an odd and in a muted way fantastic talent, as is perhaps necessary in modern English writers who manage to escape the rather stifling conditions of normal contemporary competence."[18] The critical praise is reflected in an abundance of nominations and awards. She received Booker Prize nominations for *The Dressmaker, The Bottle Factory Outing, An Awfully Big Adventure, Every Man for Himself, Master Georgie*, and *According to Queeney*. She received the Whitbread Award for *Injury Time* and *Every Man for Himself*, the Guardian Fiction Award for *The Bottle Factory Outing*, and the W. H Smith Fiction Prize for *Master Georgie*; and she won the Author of the Year Award at the British Book Awards in 1999. In addition to the television scripts she wrote for the BBC productions of *Sweet William* and *A Quiet Life*, Bainbridge has seen two of her novels, *The Dressmaker* and *An Awfully Big Adventure*, adapted into feature films.

Despite the celebrity, Bainbridge has received little attention from scholars. Beyond a handful of journal articles, only one study of her fiction has been published. Examining the "apparent mimetic simplicity" and "apparent lack of meaning" in Bainbridge's novels, Elisabeth Wennö's 1993 study, *Ironic Formula in the Novels of Beryl Bainbridge*, addresses the "permeating irony" within her novels and strives to remedy the "academic neglect" of the author via a complex theoretical interpretive matrix.[19] It is not Wennö alone who queries Bainbridge's peculiar reputation. Whereas interviewer John F. Baker takes note of the "oddball reputation that seems to cling to her,"[20] in *Contemporary British Novelists* Nick Rennison surveys the author's career and speculates on the relationship between her public image and status as a minor author:

> Beryl Bainbridge's public persona, increasingly revealed in interviews and newspaper profiles during the past ten years, is that of a quirky and lovable eccentric, pardonably over-fond of wine and cigarettes. Whatever value this persona has for Bainbridge as a private individual, it does a disservice to

her fiction. It makes it easier to sideline her work, to char-
acterize it as offbeat and oddball. It sometimes disguises
the fact that she is one of the most skilled of contemporary novelists—ruthlessly unsentimental, darkly funny and
possessed of her own unique vision of the variety and vanity
of human nature.[21]

Though readers discovering only Bainbridge's recent publica-
tions would be correct in identifying her as principally an
author of historical novels, such a view would be limited
because beginning with *A Weekend with Claud* (1967) and
continuing on until *An Awfully Big Adventure* (1989), the
majority of the author's work was not focused on remote historical eras. Although a new direction, the historical fiction
does not signal a complete departure; traits of her historical
novels—whether set in Victorian Liverpool or London in the
Augustan age—are easily detected in the earlier novels. In
short, although Bainbridge's change of genre may appear to
imply a change of theme or interests, there is in fact substantial
continuity between *A Weekend with Claud* and *According to
Queeney*.[22] In particular, Bainbridge's affinity for and transformation of the social novel, commonly identified as a key genre
in the British novelistic tradition since Austen, can be seen as
foundational in her oeuvre. In *The Modern British Novel* Malcolm Bradbury states that Bainbridge's novels from the 1970s
are "rooted in commonplace realism" and concludes that Bainbridge's "gift is to normalize and domesticate the world of
strangeness and violence, while at the same time undomesticating what we think of as the family novel."[23] In short, by introducing "strangeness and violence" into her portrayal of the
social fabric, Bainbridge alters the purview of the social novel
and darkens the image of the society to which the novel refers.

Like Bradbury, Dominic Head in his survey of British fiction from 1950 to 2000 pays close attention to the social novel and, accordingly, focuses its brief discussion of Bainbridge on her novels from the 1970s. In Head's view, novels like *The Bottle Factory Outing* and *A Quiet Life* are prime examples of the social novel, a form concerning itself with contemporary social life and "close observation of social mores"; he champions it not only because of its conventionality but also because it engages with the present, affording a "reinvigorating perspective on the real" and assisting reader "comprehension of the individual's ongoing role in social history."[24] Although there is no doubt that each Bainbridge novel closely examines social mores, the ones set in contemporary times are particularly notable for their attention to the manic vicissitudes of interpersonal relations. The dynamics of interaction within families (*The Dressmaker, A Quiet Life, An Awfully Big Adventure*) and groups of friends (*A Weekend with Claude, Another Part of the Wood, Winter Garden, Harriet Said*), as well as those between colleagues (*The Bottle Factory Outing*) and lovers (*Injury Time, Sweet William*), form the core of Bainbridge's novelistic concerns before the turn to social history that began with *Young Adolf.*

Bainbridge's examination of British society is tempered by what Bradbury calls the "frankly comic" and Rennison identifies as the "darkly funny" perspective that pervades her fiction. That broad comic sensibility, part of a tradition that Peter Ackroyd claims "has persisted in England for more than a thousand years," also relates directly to the "undomesticating" quality of the novels.[25] In contrast to the somber societal analysis offered in the social novels of her contemporaries Margaret Drabble and A. S. Byatt, a Bainbridge novel characteristically veers away from extensive moral deliberation, offering in its stead images, characters, and situations that encourage laughter—*varieties* of laughter that range from amused and derisive to mordant and despairing. The fatuous, bumbling, self-deceiving, and unlikable protagonist of *Winter Garden* and the equally self-deceiving and weak protagonist of *Injury Time*, for instance, encourage mirthful responses because their ethical lapses and sheer foolishness are freely, even extravagantly, punished. Less comfortably, though, the deaths, misery, and discord that mark the conclusions of *Another Part of the Wood*, *The Bottle Factory Outing*, and *An Awfully Big Adventure* are caused by similar social lapses and personal shortcomings. If their concluding scenes suggest lamentable tragedy, Bainbridge's tone and resolute distance from her players does not encourage amused laughter so much as coax an uneasy degree of amusement at the ridiculousness of circumstances caused by irremediably foolish and compromised people in a world of apparently random punishments and rewards.

Bainbridge's comedy, then, is not especially joyful, nor is it dedicated to dramatizing social renewal as in the romantic comedy tradition. Its dark view accords securely with Louis Kronenberger's identification of the genre's basic aim: "Comedy is concerned with human imperfection, with people's failure to measure up either to the world's or to their own conception of excellence."[26] If the critical component of comedy is conventionally tied in counterpoint to the restorative, Bainbridge's variation retains a consistent focus on human fallibility and foolishness, and on the world's violence. In her brief essay "How I Began," Bainbridge recalls rereading *Filthy Lucre* years after she had written it, and in doing so she reveals an integral aspect of her esthetic: "I also feel that I must have had a macabre sense of humour, because the best bits [of the novella]—personally speaking—have to do with either death or murder."[27] These "best bits," murder and death, are visible throughout much of her fiction of the 1970s and early 1980s. Likewise for the "awful bits about prisons and slums" that she remembers admiring in Dickens, locating analogous "bits" in any Bainbridge novel is never difficult, beginning with the vitriol, misanthropy, and gunfire of *A Weekend with Claude*.[28] Even her later historical fiction—from the account of a famed Victorian murder case in *Watson's Apology* to depictions of the doomed Scott expedition, the *Titanic* disaster, and carnage of the Crimean War—showcases numerous "awful bits" that expose a darkly comic fictional universe in which death and decay are pushed to the foreground and often linked to the egregious moral lapses or chronic and often fatal miscommunication of its characters.

Although that macabre sensibility, which initially led to Bainbridge gaining attention as a writer of thrillers,[29] may link the author to the long history of English sensation fiction, it also decisively places the novels, and in particular the early- and midcareer domestic dramas, in the comic genre. Bainbridge's humor can best be understood as black, insofar as its prevailing sentiment reflects fatalistic despair (and paradoxical mirthfulness) about the cruelty or caprice of existence and the seemingly incurable if not innate foolishness, deceit, malice, spitefulness, and fallibility of women and men. Such a perspective is evident throughout all her fiction, from *A Weekend with Claude* through *According to Queeney*. The perspective accords closely to what Patrick O'Neill calls in *The Comedy of Entropy* "the humour of uncertainty, lost norms, lost confidence, the humour of disorientation."[30]

At first glance characterizing Bainbridge as a comic novelist may seem counterintuitive insofar as that categorical definition might imply that although there may be a critical component to her novels' comic vision, there is also a fundamental orientation toward dramatizing affirmative social renewal and celebrating communality—even as she acknowledges human foibles. Yet the sheer elasticity of the comic genre allows for an enormous variety of perspectives within it. For instance, before Christopher Herbert asserts that the "genre's primordial fixation [is] on *pleasure*," he surveys the field's eminent minds and concludes that theorizing has "generated a wealth of intriguing insights but has failed to reach even the beginnings of a consensus on the defining properties of the comic."[31] Scholarship has nonetheless pointed out general tendencies in the genre. Though a simplification, its innate polar attributes or boundaries might be called negative and positive. The familiar "feel-good" modality, made familiar through romantic comedies, is marked by benign criticism and resolute optimism. Bainbridge's fiction features little of such positive and reassuring comedy, though there is much that is apparently derisive, cynical, and alienated. Commonplace in twentieth-century literature, this comic attitude functions, O'Neill claims, as "a metaphor for the crumbling of ordered systems, the breakdown of traditional perceptions of reality, the erosion of certainty" and is notable for its characteristic "blend of nihilism and humour."[32] Similarly, Alice Rayner's *Comic Persuasion* places this dualism in comedy on a utopian-to-dystopian scale, the two poles effectively aiming, respectively, to "affirm and celebrate" or "diagnose and criticize."[33] Given the preponderance of murders, immorality, decay, entrenched hostilities, failures, misunderstandings, and misdeeds (and scarcity of happiness, festivity, success, progress, and communalism) in her work, situating Bainbridge at that negative/dystopian pole satisfies logic. If, as Rayner posits, the dystopian vision "demands that we see the world as it is, which is often the same as seeing what is wrong with it,"[34] Bainbridge's social novels depict over and again what is wrong with "the world," a term that includes individuality, family dynamics, gender role limitations, British social restrictions, and even the malign indifference of the cosmos.

Overall, furthermore, Bainbridge takes two broad approaches with her dystopian comic narratives. In novels such as *Winter Garden, Young Adolf,* and *Injury Time,* for example, the plot mechanics are often farcical, showcasing an extended series of mishaps, unfortunate coincidences, and fateful accidents that befall a protagonist whose ethical lapses and unconvincing rationalizations signal his status as a target of mockery and derision. Although the hapless antihero makes efforts to wrest control over his unsatisfying circumstance, his effort results in an increasingly nightmarish episode with final scenes that offer resolution only in the sense that the novel ends. In such comedy the world of events seemingly conspires to confound the protagonist's desire for solace from the trappings of an onerous conventionality. The simple dinner party that the protagonist in *Injury Time* attends in order to appease his mistress, for instance, is disrupted and undermined by a steady series of improbable events that culminates in a hostage taking and subsequent stand off with the police. The hero's eventual—and literal—ejection from a speeding car is comic insofar as readers witness a figure of mirthful derision whose failings and lack of awareness of his own lapses seemingly invite punishment and expulsion from the social order. Likewise, in *Winter Garden* a morally compromised married man's clandestine vacation with his mistress in Soviet Russia begins with minor worries—lost luggage, mistaken identities, and unpleasant travel companions. The troubled protagonist's discomforts and anxieties increase steadily, and in the novel's concluding scene the continuance of his very life appears uncertain. As with his counterpart in *Injury Time*, the guiltily cheating middle-class husband in *Winter Garden* is held up as a target; his punishment by circumstances cast upon him by malignant and capricious world forces is intimately tied to his personal choice to accompany his mistress.

In other novels, such as *The Dressmaker, The Bottle Factory Outing, Sweet William, Another Part of the Wood*, and *An Awfully Big Adventure*, the comedy cannot be described as enjoyably mirthful. In depicting a decaying world of fractured relationships, it is resolutely despairing, aligned closely with O'Neill's comedy of entropy with its attendant alienation and joyless laughter. Individuals in these novels are hampered by personal shortcomings, economic hardships, social restrictions, and family history. Moreover the salient features of the novels —in particular, murders and deaths in *The Dressmaker, The Bottle Factory Outing, Another Part of the Wood*, and *An Awfully Big Adventure,* and marital, romantic, and familial discord in them all—establish the tendencies of the cosmological system itself as generally stultifying, often tipping toward anarchic dissolution or stifling stasis. In fact, given the preponderance of miserable characters, relationships, circumstances, and narrative resolutions, "comic" may seem an altogether erroneous label. But recall that since Aristotle the comic genre has been associated with derisive laughter resulting from the mockery of human fallibility and fatuousness and that, more recently, black comedy—the "diagnostic and critical" dystopian comedy of Rayner, the "entropic" humor of O'Neill—

has placed a mirthless, despairing, and befuddled laughter-response in the foreground.

Lastly the comic aspect of Bainbridge's novels—ranging from the relatively benign ridicule of a romantic relationship in *Sweet William* to the frequent mordant depictions of failed friendships, romance, family, community, and individual growth (all set in a world that conspires to orchestrate mishaps while limiting opportunities for its inhabitants) that begin with *A Weekend with Claude*—is evident not only because of the ridiculousness and ludicrousness of character and situation but also because of the frequent mocking distance of the narrative perspective. *The Bottle Factory Outing* offers a good example. The novel depicts an idyllic situation—a bucolic picnicking outing for a small group of employees of a London wine-bottling company that offers personal and professional opportunities for its two protagonists. It concludes with Freda, the would-be social climbing aspirant of the pair, being killed and then stuffed by her colleagues into a soon-to-be-exported liquor barrel. Reader unease and dismay at the circumstances before and after her death are tempered and redirected by Bainbridge's antic plot and antipathetic characterization; although a protagonist's death could elicit concern, the ludicrousness of Freda's situation and the exorbitance of her unlikable traits ultimately incite more mirth than outrage or horror. The intensity or presence of this misanthropic, dark-hued comedy varies from novel to novel but remains constant throughout many of Bainbridge's novels of domestic drama.

Despite her statement in *English Journey* that the "past is a foreign country. Its pavements are haunted by people who speak a language we don't understand," Bainbridge's recent novels have been exclusively interested in the topography of the British past.[35] Set in England or during English enterprises at sea or land, these novels—*Young Adolf, Watson's Apology, The Birthday Boys, Every Man for Himself, Master Georgie*, and *According to Queeney*—have depicted the tumultuous lives of English characters during the reigns of George (III, V) and Victoria. And though it could be argued that Bainbridge has been preoccupied with English history since childhood (after all, *Filthy Lucre* opens on "a murky evening in 1851"),[36] it was only with the publication of *Young Adolf* (1978) that she publicly expressed this interest. Since 1978, in fact, she has seldom scrutinized contemporary England in her fiction, apparently preferring to no longer abide by publisher and friend Anna Haycroft's longstanding advice to her: "Write about what you know."[37] "I felt I'd used up my childhood in all the other books," Bainbridge has stated in explanation of her shift to historical inquiry.[38]

Like her unconventional exploration of the social novel form, Bainbridge's undertakings in historical fiction cannot be classified simply. To a degree, her novels can be described as classical historical fiction. They strive, in short, to portray realistically historical moments, figures, and epochs with apparent factual fidelity. This dedication, as Avrom Fleishman observes, is a core principle of serious historical fiction: "Yet the value and, almost inevitably, the meaning of a historical novel will stand in some relation to the habitual demand for truth, and it is here that a theory of the genre needs to begin."[39] And although Fleishman acknowledges that historical novelists necessarily tell their story with invented details, they are nonetheless fundamentally reliant on principles that also guide any historiography aiming to recover the past: "The historical novelist provokes or conveys, by imaginative sympathy, the *sentiment de l'existence*, the feeling of how it was to live in another age. To do this he must describe and interpret—more or less accurately—the states of affairs that called forth the personal responses of the kind he wishes to portray."[40] Bainbridge explicitly adheres to this notion of accuracy of interpretation. In the author's note prefacing *Watson's Apology*, for example, she explains that the novel seeks to fill in the character motivation, conversations, and feeling that "defeated historical inquiry."[41]

In other ways Bainbridge's historical novels are not so readily classified as being dedicated to pursuing an empirical or objective historical truth. In fact their highlighting of partial knowledge, subjective and individual perspective, and marginal voices links them to literary postmodernity. This facet of her historical novels also coincides with a widespread literary turning to history from the 1980s onward, as evidenced by novels by Peter Ackroyd, A. S. Byatt, Caryl Phillips, Jeanette Winterson, John Fowles, Timothy Mo, Julian Barnes, Margaret Drabble, and Nigel Williams. Margaret Scanlan argues that this discomforting postmodern counterpart of the conventional historical novel "emphasizes the difficulties of knowing the truth about the past."[42] Such fiction, also identified by Linda Hutcheon as "historiographic metafiction" in *A Poetics of Postmodernism*, asserts its commitment to illuminating acts of historical representation even as it announces a fundamental skepticism about our ability to do so given ideological bias, limitations of systems of discourse, and the textual basis of our ostensible knowledge of the past itself. Bainbridge's fractured or multiple narratives in *The Birthday Boys*, *Master Georgie*, and *According to Queeney*, patently fabulous invention in *Young Adolf*, and "decentered"[43] perspectives, especially in *Master Georgie* and *The Birthday*

Boys, temper "known truths" of historical events such as the Crimean War, the *Titanic* disaster, and the Scott expedition to the South Pole. If they do not subvert or self-consciously call attention to their own narrative reliability or dedicate pages to recuperating "lost" points of view and those underrepresented by historiography, the partiality, marginality, and plurality of the novels' narrative voices do effectively direct concentration on the disjuncture between fictive representation and the putative factuality of British history.

CHAPTER 2

Opening Strategies
A Weekend with Claude, Another Part of the Wood, and *Harriet Said*

I was alive during the war. What happened to the Jews
changed me forever.

Beryl Bainbridge, *Paris Review,* Winter 2000

With her first three novels, *A Weekend with Claud* (1967),
Another Part of the Wood (1968), and *Harriet Said* (1972),
Beryl Bainbridge introduced readers to the elements of the imaginary topography—dark views on human motivation and capa-
bility, episodic plot delineation, and subtly comic regard for the
vicissitudes and caprice of the universe—that would be characteristic of all of her subsequent social novels, from *The Dressmaker* to *An Awfully Big Adventure*. To a degree these early
novels have been disavowed by Bainbridge; dissatisfied with the
initial pair, in fact, she revised them, republishing *Another Part
of the Wood* in 1979 and *A Weekend with Claude* in 1981.
Despite the author's dismissal, the novels are far from atypical.[1]
In featuring small groups in relative isolation; characters with
notably limited compassion and excessive senses of self-worth,
vanity, and spite; antagonistic interactions; a background of
decay and aesthetic blight; and plot developments that do not
point to the conventional ameliorative "eventual reconciliation"
of individual and society (as John Richetti has written of in his

history of the British novel),[2] the novels are emblematic insofar as they exhibit key Bainbridge traits and trajectories.

Moreover surveying these novels and their depictions of intelligence without compassion or moral compass, social groupings often bereft of affection, commonplace misunderstandings that result in excessive actions based on these misunderstandings, and social conventions as oppressive and restrictive forces (with no alternative offered in their place) also reveals traces of Bainbridge's comic regard for character and social context. Those elements of black comedy that pervade the novels—or as David Punter calls them, the "fables of psychosis"[3]—of the 1970s (with 1977's *Injury Time* the farcical high mark) are most evident here in the form of distancing; the frequent grotesquerie of Bainbridge's characters clearly marks them as comic antagonists or as ridiculous figures of mirth, though not necessarily as jolly or funny. Overall the characters' lack of redeeming qualities and the plot's unwillingness to grant development to characters or their social environment—typically no epiphany sets characters on the right path, no flexibility allows society to develop or change— establishes Bainbridge as a satirist. Readers may be appalled at the characters' exorbitant vanity and transparent scheming, or they may laugh at the fanciful imaginings and risible self-delusions, but they are rarely placed in the position of empathizing with them and their plight in the world. Scenes of death, violence, and dissolution, lastly, are suggestive of the grave "entropic" comedy discussed by O'Neill, its satiric goals not weighted in favor of the normative and ameliorative but, rather, to the anomic; instead of being "judicial, regulative, prescriptive," Bainbridge's fiction is "descriptive, observational, revelatory, apocalyptic, voyeuristic."[4] As such, its gimlet-eyed critical assessment offers little solace or indication of future progress, the remote, observational point of view less dedicated to speculating about means to repair the damage than to simply depicting its facets.

A Brief Gathering of Acquaintances: *A Weekend with Claude*

While the widely rejected manuscript of *Harriet Said* (completed in 1958) was the first novel Bainbridge wrote, she regarded her second attempt and first published novel, *A Weekend with Claud* (1967), as a failure. That she published a revised version, *A Weekend with Claude*, in 1981 suggests that the initial failure was not irremediable.[5] Although the novel was not widely reviewed, those few critics praised it while citing faults. The unsigned review in the *Times Literary Supplement*, for example, noted that the "writing is sound and professional" but the novel's "fatal fault" results in the interest being "dissipated over too many people and their relationships are not clearly enough defined." The *New York Review of Books* reviewer related Bainbridge to Henry Green, "that specialist in inconsequentialities and longueurs," and judged the novel to be "wonderfully alert to the flow of feeling between friends" despite flaws of execution. The *Listener* review contended that Bainbridge could "clearly write a better novel when she finds a more robust theme" but also concluded that her debut "overworks the filmic technique of fading and focus" and produces "mannered ambiguity" that is "too obscurely subjective."[6]

In both versions the novel comprises seven chapters, four of which are set in the novel's present day and take up only a small fraction of the total number of pages. In those brief chapters a married couple visits the farmhouse of Claude and Julia Perkins and engage in an awkward and occasionally tense conversation with Claude, who operates an antiques business from his home. While selecting a desk, the visiting woman discovers a letter and a photograph in its drawer. Claude explains it is "merely an old letter [of his friend Lily's] and a photograph I took in the garden that weekend in the summer" (16).[7] The letter and photograph generate three lengthy first-person accounts of that weekend by individuals captured on film, titled "Lily," "Victorian Norman," and "Shebah." By revealing the fractious relations among the ostensible friends—the high point of which is the supposedly accidental shooting of Shebah by Claude—and the remarkable self-absorption and vitriol of each character, Bainbridge fabricates astonishing character portraits and comments on the unreliability of both memory and human perception. Furthermore, by juxtaposing the polite conversation between aggressive, bohemian Claude and the decorum-bound middle-class couple in the present, Bainbridge draws attention to the falsity and tensions of social relations in general.

The brief chapters set in the novel's present day emphasize the tension between antagonistic, occasional bully Claude and the married couple, who decide to purchase the desk that contains the letter and photograph. Claude's behavior, apparently designed to provoke or taunt the convention-minded couple, aggravates the male and embarrasses the female. Initially, however, Bainbridge's portrayal of Claude is sympathetic. He married the highly organized and thorough Julia after Sarah, his first wife, deserted him years earlier. The marital breach resulted in trauma, depression, and hospitalization, from which Julia nursed him back to health. Claude imagines his subsequent weight gain as being "the body's way of protecting itself from ever being beautiful again" (11). Bainbridge's representation soon changes in tone. The visiting customer responds to Claude's aggression and Freudian free thinking by being dismissive and angrily murmuring, "Nonsense" (14), and his wife, often consumed with embarrassment and excitement, has an ambivalent response to Claude's flattering words and sexual charisma. Their marital tension results from the threat Claude poses to the sanctity of the couple's monogamy. That tension also implicitly critiques their adherence to status quo conventions.

Examining the photograph, the woman asks, "Why are they all friends?" (96). The lengthy chapters that expose each friend present readers with unlikable and at times unbearable figures but no certain answer to her question. Through interior monologues each chapter instead reveals the disdainful attitude the characters hold toward a variety of subjects, especially the other weekend guests. Bainbridge's warts-and-all depiction of the characters' opinions and intense self-regard effectively shines a critical light on them, highlighting their flaws and weaknesses in a dramaturgical way, as though they are serially staged individual character monologues.

Lily, for example, is Claude's long-established friend. Since Claude already knows the "pain of unrequited love," Lily relies on him to "persuade [her paramours] to love her properly" (17). The focus of attention of Claude, Victorian Norman, and Shebah, Lily's perspectives and experiences are represented in the first (and briefest) interior monologue of *A Weekend with Claude*. Beginning with the phrase "I don't know whether I've had a nice time or not" (18), the chapter's characterization of Lily reveals an insecure and vacillating woman—often worried about being unattractive and losing her eligibility for love and marriage—whose thoughts about the other weekend guests of Claude are as indecisive as the question she asks herself: "I am here . . . but who am I?" (34). The weekend is "terrifically important" for Lily because she believes that she is pregnant (by Billie, who has since left her) and needs to convince Edward, her latest boyfriend, that he is the father of her child. Although the deception galls her, she deems her future security of greater importance than the technicality of mere facts. Lily's thoughts also recall an assortment of scenes from her past. The scenes are disturbing: privileged girls who were cruel to her at school, for instance; and a miserable family, which included a father with whom she physically fought and who told her that she was "a little bastard, a filthy animal with no respect, a dirty little beast who should have died in the grass" (31); and her loss of virginity: "With an adroit convulsive roll a penetration unpremeditated and untender took place" (36). She regrets the "rackety life" (32) she has led and charts the decay of love and contentment following the brief moment when she was "safe and happy and hopeful" (34).

The narrator of "Victorian Norman" reveals himself to be a self-styled iconoclast whose allegiance to the Communist Party and antiquated mode of dress draw attention to his aesthete's disposition and rebellious posture. A "martyr without a cause" who believes "in Marxist ideology and yet actively participating in the survival of capitalism" (59), the monologue of this atheist factory worker likewise reveals the complexity and hypocrisy of an extraordinarily unlikable individual. Though the reader's introduction to Victorian Norman comes via Lily—she perceives him as "awfully clever" (30), a man who is proud of his primal self (as he states, "I drink. I copulate" [38])—Norman's own sentiments expose a man who happily embraces his contradictions and chooses the immediate satisfactions of desire and impulse over the dictates of convention. The closing moment of Norman's monologue takes note of Baudelaire's aphorism

"There is nothing that is not misunderstanding" (95). That aphorism is emblematic of Norman himself, who views society as befuddled and, unlike himself, free of will and secure rationality.

Bainbridge devotes her longest chapter to the self-revelation of Shebah, the eldest of the group, born in 1899. A Jew who was persecuted during World War II, she is nonetheless an intensely disagreeable character whose vanity, sense of entitlement, and delusions of grandeur mark her as monstrous. She judges her friends and acquaintances as "dreadful fools" whose "banality robbed [her] heart of heights of happiness" (139). Perceiving herself to be an absolute outsider, neither able to adopt the weekend group's "general attitude of abandonment" (98) nor invited to partake, her monologue counterpoints her scathing views about the weekend with Claude with memories of her benighted past. Of the group members, she apparently abhors "that swine Claude" (98) (even though she later regards him, variously, as "most interesting" [113], "quite insane" [132], and "barbarous" [136]) and expresses contempt for "those jealous, petty female impersonators with their tight calculating little minds and their dependence of men" (99). Despite being called "Persecutor of Christ . . . Killer of Jesus" (98) and being hit with a brick by a bigoted neighbor, Shebah is a decidedly unsympathetic character. Juxtaposing her intelligence to the group's "pathetic bird-droppings of knowledge on books and politics and fashion" (101), Shebah repeatedly conceives of herself as innately superior to her companions, those "vermin who barely inhabit the earth" (105). Unlike the others, whom she sees as preoccupied by sex and other avenues of sublimation, Shebah states, "But I have nothing, no compensations, no curtain of deceit to hide myself from myself—only my poor brain endlessly facing itself" (118).

Compared to Lily's vacillations and Norman's solipsism, She-bah's boundless self-pity and raw misanthropic contempt for everyone signal the pathology of her character.

In the novel's brief final chapter, the married couple leaves and Claude promises to deliver the desk. He later decides to delay delivery by a week and to befriend the woman in order to "make her life more richer, more varied" (150). He returns the letter to the desk so the woman will read it and places the photograph of the three friends on the mantelpiece, where it begins to accumulate dust. The previous character monologues, exposing the falsity of the familiar summery nostalgic image, place Claude in another context and help explain his unusual behavior with the married couple. If the narrating technique of *A Weekend with Claude* is unique in Bainbridge's work, the emphasis on the misery, anger, and passion below the surface of an ostensibly benign or unexceptional event or place is a mainstay. Through these portraits, moreover, Bainbridge is introducing a series of personality types that recur in her fiction. Befuddled, passive, and lovelorn Lily, for example, shares qualities with Rita in *The Dressmaker* and Ann in *Sweet William*; Claude shares qualities with Joseph in *Another Part of the Wood* and the titular figure in *Sweet William*; and although undoubtedly singular in the Bainbridge corpus, the excessive and erratic self-pity and rage of Shebah are visible as well in Freda in *The Bottle Factory Outing* and May in *Another Part of the Wood*. More than being merely *Bainbridge types*, these characters, which Bainbridge renders with the physical and mental characteristics and biographical qualities of realistic characters, reflect an apparently cynical (and at times misanthropic) vision of humanity.

Tied to this unappealing model of the human, Bainbridge draws attention as well to the specific contours of the genders.

Locked into an uncomfortable but genetically irresistible embrace, Bainbridge's heterosexual women and men feel no apparent affection or interest in one another, though their sexual and reproductive impulses draw them together. Under this biological imperative women scheme for mates who can fill their material wants and fulfill their maternal desires; men usually give little evidence of interest in monogamy or emotional commitment to their wives or lovers. (And when they do, they are weak and incapable men surrounded by or married to hectoring women.) In addition, same-sex friendships, especially between women, are rife with rivalry. In all cases the inexorable force of convention exerts itself, assuring the continuance of a social norm that satisfies no one. In offering a variety of unappealing and even repellent characters that exhibit no interest in or sign of redeeming themselves or undergoing a moral transformation, Bainbridge establishes her inaugural image of England—an apparently hard and static place and people—and her narrator's distance from it.

Rural Weekending: *Another Part of the Wood*

Bainbridge's next publication, *Another Part of the Wood* (1968), foreshadows themes and structures of her fiction throughout the 1970s and into the early 1980s.[8] *Another Part of the Wood*, like *The Dressmaker, The Bottle Factory Outing, Sweet William, A Quiet Life,* and *Injury Time,* is written in the third person and examines the fractious interactions of a small, ostensibly intimate group in an insular location. Slightly less misanthropic and pessimistic than the later fiction, the novel nonetheless emphatically draws attention to the cruelty, misunderstanding, vanity, indifference, and power struggles that permeate social relations. The novel's conclusion—featuring the accidental death of a boy as his father plays an aggressive game of Monopoly—implicates all the remaining principal characters, as though their failure to behave with dignity, respect, selflessness, and tolerance has in fact been equivalent to criminal negligence. The distant narration and often grotesque, unsympathetic characterization, moreover, convey Bainbridge's antipathetic comic perspective about these English lives. Evaluating the revised version, the reviewer in the *Spectator* noted that the "typically Bainbridgean comic scenario with undertones of violence" was muddled but worthwhile, particularly because it "emphasizes the comedy of awkwardness." The *Listener* drew attention to the deftness and restraint of Bainbridge's depiction of a "grotesque menagerie of creepies." The *New York Review of Books* compared the novel to *A Weekend with Claude* and observed that the sensitivity and nuance had improved because "it has more of a story to tell."[9]

Because *Another Part of the Wood* does not feature a highly structured plot—it is an episodic account of conversations and leisurely activities that occur during a brief getaway—its principal focus is, like *A Weekend with Claude*, portraiture. Two acquainted couples, Joseph and Dotty and Lionel and May, visit the Nant MacFarley Camp in Wales for a weekend. Despite the bucolic image (which recalls the equally illusory summertime idyll of the photograph's setting in *A Weekend with Claude*), each pairing is fraught with tension and anger. Reminiscent of Claude, Joseph is domineering, cruel, and indifferent, and his younger girlfriend Dotty is miserable, hapless, and frustrated. The marriage of Lionel and May is likewise unhappy: May resents her husband and the steady decline of his career and makes consistent efforts to belittle and hector him and to sabotage his efforts; and Lionel's constant inanity and forced cheer signal both his weakness and his Willy

Loman–like unwillingness to address his career and marital failings. Like supporting characters in a drawing-room stage comedy, Joseph's child, Roland, and ward, Kidney; the grounds-keepers, Willie and Balfour; and the property owner, George MacFarley, are reflective surfaces that provide commentary about the principals even while they are often the objects of those characters' derisive attention.

Each of the novel's ten chapters is divided into discrete episodes that record the thoughts, actions, and social intercourse of the characters. In keeping with expectation of a weekend get-away, the daily activities are largely unremarkable—members of the group play Monopoly, a wasp's nest causes unease, a small fire in a field leads to minor injury, Dottie walks with Balfour to the local village for food because she has been accused of consuming more than her share of the limited store. Less conventionally, there are continuous conflicts and disagreements between the characters and worry about possible sexual misconduct between Roland and Kidney. The physical limitations of the setting accordingly force attention on the actions of the characters as well as their thoughts and words and their psychological underpinnings. As with *A Weekend with Claude*, the characters of *Another Part of the Wood* are not models of enlightened thought or selfless behavior. Petty, self-absorbed, indifferent to others, and often cruel, their individual motivations are complex and idiosyncratic, related to, for example, asserting their superiority, airing complaints of their victimization, and maintaining the cohesion of the group at any cost.

The permanent residents of the Welsh campground, and secondary characters in the novel, are its gigantic owner, George MacFarley, whose face "manages to convey serenity and imbecility at one and the same time" (17); the elderly groundskeeper

Willie; and Edgar Balfour, a shy, stuttering young man who is self-conscious about his pitted complexion. The weekend gathering at their camp has been organized by Joseph, "arty" (51), articulate, and an opinionated aesthete who, according to his younger, embittered, and "provincial" (49) girlfriend Dotty, "thinks he's God" (18). Joseph is soon after judged by Balfour to be "the arch-conformer of all time, stereotyped, well-bred, unemotional" (10). Joseph's patronizing and critical attitude causes those with whom he interacts to recoil. Dottie, having spent intimate time with Joseph and been the subject of his withering criticism, remarks about his insincerity (claiming, for instance, "Every gesture he makes is just a monotonous repeat of a gesture he's made somewhere else" [19]) and, when he speaks yet again of his complex dreams, expresses resentment for his self-absorption about his "everlasting nights of symbolic imagery" (37). Divorced, Joseph arrives with his son Roland and Kidney, a mentally handicapped youth whose rehabilitation he has undertaken; he is remote and imperious with both youths.

Joseph has invited his acquaintance Lionel and Lionel's "restless" (51) wife, May, who arrive later that same day. Lionel is a ridiculous, pompous, and fatuous figure whose constant point of reference is the supposedly disciplined and character-building time he spent in the army—the truth of his experience is far removed from the fantasy version he fabricates for listeners. Bainbridge often renders his speech as a series of clichés, for example, "Seen all types from all walks of life, and—make no bones about it—it separates the wheat from the chaff" (55), and so highlights his unwillingness to accept the truth of his failures and his constant dedication to maintaining appearances. The incipient alcoholic Lionel is locked into a marriage with May, who goads and wounds her husband, giving him only brief and

occasional intervals of respite. When she is not belittling or publicly ridiculing him (calling Lionel "utterly grotesque" [69], for
instance, for all to hear), May endeavors to give others reason to
dislike him and have sympathy for her plight as the wife of such
a disturbed man: "Lionel cut all the stuffing out of my bra, you
know" (62), she tells Dottie, implying that she lives with a mad-
man. Despite her disdain and the multilayered dysfunction of
their unconsummated (103) yet unexpectedly sexual marital
relationship (of Lionel's eccentric sexual fantasies, May recalls
how "he mouthed those dreadful words into her brain as if he
were demented" [59]), May commits to a marriage whose basis
perplexes her:

> It was stupid really, because all the time she was screaming
> at him she did know fractionally that he was good and sin-
> cere and normal—yes, even normal in a way—and that he
> was light years away from people like Joseph, superior in
> every way. Yet she couldn't tell him. She hated him for his
> rolling belly and the bald patch on his head and the way he
> would go on about the army, and deep down, way down,
> she was frightened of him and of what he thought of her.
> He didn't even know her, and she couldn't explain herself
> how she had come to marry this stranger with the thinning
> hair. (58)

Bainbridge contrasts May's worldliness and cynicism with
Lionel's comically if pathetically deluded misperception of his
wife, whom he sees as "so innocent" (81), a "little flower" and
a "child" (73). Within this fantasy, he sees himself as May's pro-
tector from a reality about which her putative innocence acts as
shield: "The world was a deep deceptive forest, full of promises
and little glades and clearings, and in the dark depths roamed the
wolves, savage, snapping their great teeth, waiting to spring on

those who wandered from the path. May was so unaware of the dark places, so trusting, so unconscious of danger" (73). Despite her belief in her own exceptional insight, May seems incapable of extricating herself from the confines of marriage. Instead she lashes out—revealing, for instance, that she had an extramarital affair, not to confide so much as to cause pain—and when she locates her husband's much-valued coin memento (which he found in a urinal but tells people he heroically took "from around the neck of a German officer in Italy" [101]), she discards it. This latter act, which Lionel hears about from Roland, is a catalyst for his eventual change of attitude from love for May to disdain; it is this increased polarization that stands in place as the novel reaches its conclusion.

If Bainbridge depicts romantic unions as tense entanglements, she also represents friendships as fraught; they offer little support and few benefits. The men, for example, compete for leadership with one another or simply exert the dominant facets of their personalities, Joseph typically censorious and dismissive and Lionel appeasing and full of forced bonhomie. Communalism is never easily reached; nor is it enduring. Solidarity and friendships are either ephemeral or trivial, and group mirthfulness comes at the expense of others. Bonds frequently shift, too. When Dottie and May share a rare moment of seemingly heartening laughter ("They both started to laugh—Dotty loudly, with her mouth wide open and her two feet set in a circlet of sunshine, May with pinks lips compressed and shoulders wriggling" [62]), it is in response to Lionel's ridiculousness. Yet "huge and vicious with hunger" (93), Dottie hours later agrees with Balfour's disparaging assessment of May, Lionel, and Joseph as unfathomable or crazy, adding, "They're all barmy" (95). Later still, when May sees evidence of Dottie's pubic hair escaping from the edge of her swimsuit, she feels deep revulsion, "almost nausea," and thinks, "Other women were always revolting" (128).

In addition to depicting undesirable Hogarthian figures and anatomizing the romantic bonds and social intercourse of this small group of weekenders, discourse in *Another Part of the Wood* undertakes the form of dispersed dialogue, speculating about or expounding on the nature of existence. Since the ideas originate from single characters and are not often shared as conversation within the world of the novel, this dialogue does not benefit or contribute to the weekend community at Nant Mac-Farley Camp. The reader is the sole audience, gleaning from individual characters' thoughts and voiced perspectives worldviews that accept (or at least expect) the fragility, uncertainty, and absurdity of human life.

The vision that Bainbridge develops relates closely to the "disturbing" nature of entropic comedy as delineated by O'Neill:[10] George's exposure to the odd behavior of the group the night before also pushes him to decide that "nothing was entirely accidental nor entirely planned. Chaos could escalate to such a point that what preceded it achieved a degree of order" (91–92). When he later turns to Tolstoy in order to note that "life is all right while you are intoxicated" but that once "you sober up it's possible not to see it's a fraud" (121), Joseph retorts with an aphoristic statement from Marlon Brando: "Nothing lasts, absolutely nothing. Neither fear, nor love for one woman" (121). Dottie's comment to Balfour, "Joseph says my hunger means something else. . . . But then everything means something else, doesn't it?" (107), adds to these ideas of impermanence, questioning the certainty of both communication and rational motivation. Balfour later returns to Dottie's observation, recalling, "Behind everything, they said, lay something else, another

meaning altogether." And yet from what he sees as the antitradi-
tional philosophical beliefs of Joseph and the others emerges
their alienation. For Balfour "there wasn't anything else" besides
loyalty to kin; and because men like George and Joseph do not
"really feel that they belonged to anyone anymore" (145), they
are no longer tethered to social verities and become, for Balfour,
unintelligible. Joseph, an adherent of Freud, pays attention to
dreams because "the mind is less inhibited when we sleep": "We
can be our true selves then—give vent to all kinds of repressed
desires, act out our fantasies, behave without the restraints im-
posed by society" (94). Complementing these insights about
human nature and life, Bainbridge frequently patterns conversation to highlight the gaps, the misunderstandings, and limits of
communication between individuals. For example, when Dottie
confides to May that Joseph is physically disgusted by her, "May
tried to express sympathy and incredulity, but was too absorbed
in her make-up, barely listening to the girl" (104). The self-
absorption of May is typical for her, and repetition of that style
of oddly noninteractive interaction is a frequent characteristic of
the social intercourse within Bainbridge's fiction.

Another Part of the Wood concludes on the final day of the
weekend and with the playing of a second game of Monopoly.
Kissed by Balfour after she has nursed him through an epileptic
seizure, Dottie abruptly decides to leave Joseph and Nant Mac-
Farley Camp, "glad to be free—if not yet emotionally, then
geographically" (152). Her action, a determined rejection of
decorous propriety that is an unusual occurrence in Bainbridge's
fiction, barely registers with Joseph and is regarded as theatrical
and silly by the others. The remaining adults, meanwhile, having
satisfied themselves that Joseph's son Roland was not sexually
molested by Kidney earlier in the day, remain nonetheless

unaware that the child's sluggish behavior is a result of his over-ingestion of Kidney's sedative medication. Lionel, having been informed by Roland that May discovered his missing war memento and threw it into a wasp's nest, finds his heart hardening, experiencing "a prolapse of feeling beyond adjustment" that causes him to recall his father's "righteous mouth" and "similar unrelenting eyes gazing at him without understanding" (156). While Lionel inspects the sleeping child (and feels a "stab of dislike" for him, so like his father, "a natural beast of the forest") and reports him "sleeping peacefully" (156), Balfour's visit a short time later culminates with the final, stuttered words of the novel: "He's d-dead" (159). Alone with the apparently over-dosed child, Balfour's nihilistic epiphany (with its conclusion: "He was nothing really" [158]) serves as a complement to Lionel's resignation and a contrast to Dottie's breaking away from the oppression of her relationship with Joseph:

> He couldn't feel surprised or shocked. He had always, it seemed, been on the threshold of some experience that would open a door, and now here was just such an experience and there was no sudden illumination, no revelation such as he had imagined. Indeed it appeared to him that the door had closed for ever. He was quite untouched, it wasn't his loss. He should, like a man drowning, relive his gone-through life, but he couldn't do it. There were no pictures, no truths, no emotions. Soon, in a few hours, he knew there would be an ambulance and a general exodus, a dispersal into the landscape, a journey into another part of the wood. (158)

These final images—a preventable death, fractured relationships, the failure of community, and an indifferent "dispersal into the landscape"—signal both Balfour's despairing alienation and more generally a summarizing encapsulation of existence within the novel. It depicts an absurd world of largely meaningless but intact and coercive conventions that is for the most part populated by selfish and wounded (yet often hurtful) individuals fated never to grow.

Our Summer Vacation: *Harriet Said*

Harriet Said (1972) did not meet with immediate success. Submitted to an assortment of publishers in the early 1960s, it was rejected because it was judged to be technically of merit but also an ethically irresponsible treatment of weighty material and as such undeserving of publication.[11] George Braziller, the eventual American publisher of *Harriet Said*, included telling remarks on the dust jacket from an unnamed editor at the rival publisher who had rejected the early manuscript: "Your writing shows considerable promise, but what repulsive little creatures you have made the two central characters, repulsive almost beyond belief. And I think the scene in which the two men and the two girls meet in the Tsar's house is too indecent and unpleasant even for these lax days."[12] The comment is fascinating insofar as it underscores the publisher's need for authorial judgment of the characters, if not a charting of their eventual rehabilitation—a need Bainbridge does not share. Reviewers noted the changing mores between Bainbridge's first publication attempt circa 1958 and success circa 1972 and generally focused on the novel's variety of merits. The *New York Time Book Review* stated that the novel "certainly ranks in content with the more celebrated thrillers of corrupt childhood, but it has literary and psychological virtues as well." The *Spectator* reviewer took note of the "totally convincing" portraiture and "beautifully described" pathology before his concluding comment that the novel is a "thoroughly enjoyable horror experience." Whereas the brief *Times Literary Supplement* review called *Harriet Said* a "very good first third novel indeed," Karl Miller in the *New York Review of Books* wondered about the goal of the "absorbing" but "a little incoherent" novel: "Bainbridge is sometimes neglectful of her responsibility toward the reader, who needs more nursing than he receives." Furthermore, Miller said, "It may be that a question arises concerning the violent deaths she is apt to inflict, as here. Is she really a writer of thrillers, of what Graham Greene regards as entertainments—fashionably black ones at that?"[13]

Similar to her two earlier novels, the novel's apparent placidity belies a disturbing depth. In fact the idyllic setting of *Harriet Said*—generically a coming-of-age narrative in which two teenaged girls spend the last of their summer vacation together at an English seaside town—disguises pervasive moral corruption and criminal behavior. Elisabeth Wennö points to the probable Freudian[14] interpretation of the relationships before addressing what she contends is Bainbridge's broader concern: "The novel asserts the existential truth of the myth of the fall, exposes the shortcomings of mental creation, and points to shared acceptance as redemption."[15] She concludes that Bainbridge holds a "pessimistic view" because of her "emphasis on entrapment and separation as inescapable conditions of life."[16] Though the two protagonists may well be regarded as "repulsive little creatures," Bainbridge's vision broadens the scope of the repellent to include an apparently upright neighbor and ordinary law-abiding individuals, such as the girls' parents. As with the previous novels, too, the moral codes governing behavior are corroded, distorted, or subverted. In *Harriet Said*, Bainbridge changes emphasis: the might-be accidental shooting of Shebah in

A Weekend with Claude and the overdose death of Roland in *Another Part of the Wood*—passive acts that ultimately reflect character indifference, vanity, and self-absorption—are followed in *Harriet Said* by a spontaneous murder, an active decision that asserts character disavowal of a significant conventional moral code.

Capturing the seemingly benign misadventure of two girls at home from school for summer vacation, the novel's brief, prologuelike first chapter depicts the narrator and her intimate friend Harriet running across a field at night, rehearsing responses they will give to their parents following an undisclosed crime. Harriet assures the narrator, "It was his fault. We are not to blame" (7) and then utters, in apparent exaltation, "terrible long drawn out sounds that pierced the darkness" (8). The subsequent fourteen chapters chronicle the minor events that lead up to that nocturnal calamity. Episodic and structured as though to emulate the meandering and unplanned days of summer vacation, the novel offers an account of the daily life of the precocious thirteen-year-old narrator. In addition to the account of her ideas, feelings, and activities, the unnamed narrator describes her complex friendship with her best friend Harriet, elder by one year.

The girl is given to wandering far from her family, her observant nature drawn to cataloging unseemly sights and unusual events. For instance, she recalls, "There were no end of things Harriet and I had found. Whole crates of rotten fruit, melons and oranges and grapefruits, swollen up and bursting with salt water, lumps of meat wrapped in stained cotton sheets through which the maggots tunneled if the weather was warm, and stranded jelly fish, purple things, obscene and mindless" (17). Besides a sighting of excrement and a fantasy of discovering a dead baby "still in a bag of skin on its side in the mud" (18), the narrator regularly encounters and delights in engaging with grotesque locals like an "awful" and "dreadful" priest with "fingers stained up to the knuckle with nicotine" (18), a "senile" canon, and Perjer, a "lost soul" (137) who is a notorious alcoholic village recluse rumored to be a pederast. The narrator's intellectual project—the attainment of this specialized type of knowledge—is also a private undertaking, shared by Harriet but unknown to all others.

The narrator is observant enough to comprehend that she is unusual and abnormal. At the beginning of the novel she admits to being irritable and bored without her friend because she has no others. She confides that she is a "special case" and "a disgrace owing to the dirty stories found in my notebook" (10). Considered out of control and in need of supervision, the girl believes her parents truly fear the intimacy of her friendship with Harriet. And although her attitude generally presupposes that she and Harriet are superior in every way to their families and members of the community, she has occasional regrets about her outsider's perspective, such as, for instance, when she sees her younger sister and concludes, "I did not want her to be like us. God willing she would grow up normally and be like everyone else" (16). Even so, Bainbridge portrays the girls (and the narrator in particular) as being in many ways ordinary teenagers, subject to the usual teenagers' secretiveness, ennui ("I just wanted something to happen" [18], the narrator complains), self-examining uncertainties (the pensive narrator is prone to question herself as desirable: "I was thirteen but I looked ancient beside Harriet, with my permed hair and plump body" [32]), and emotional volatility (tempestuous love follows quickly after intense hatred, and ecstatic laughter is soon transformed into tears). The narrator's declaration, "I stood there mutely, crying endlessly in distress, not knowing why" (56), is reiterated with slight variation several times throughout the novel.

In addition to that depiction of conventionally anguished adolescence, Bainbridge's characterization highlights the girls' eccentric philosophy of experience, which recalls the esthetic hedonism of Walter Pater as well as the notorious Leopold and Loeb murder case of 1924 (treated on screen in Alfred Hitchcock's *Rope* [1948], Richard Fleischer's *Compulsion* [1959], Tom Kalin's *Swoon* [1992], and Michael Haneke's *Funny Games* [1997]). The philosophy of the girls involves a repeated pretense of being conventional and normal and, accordingly, acting shocked or surprised or amused when they know that convention dictates they should be. Harriet, for example, "is fond of assuming the character expected of her in certain different houses" (46). Likewise, when the narrator says, "We both tried very hard to give our parents love, and security, but they were too demanding" (35), she acknowledges both the limits of her bond with her parents and the need for artifice to maintain her appearance as a dutiful and loving daughter. Their worldview necessitates this posture. The girls in fact see themselves as supremely logical scientific observers who are detached from the banality, ugliness, and moral limitations of their families and community. The narrator recalls the thrill of being called a "dirty little angel" (37) by an Italian prisoner and recognizes, a year later, that "it was not enough; more elaborate things had to be said; each new experience had to leave a more complicated tracery of sensations; to satisfy us every memory must be more desperate than the last" (38). Her brief history of their search for "experience" and "information"—"of the things [the narrator] had done" (39) since the prisoner's comment—which Harriet identifies as a kind of rational and dispassionate training course for adult life (39), would, the narrator believes, rank as perverse "enormities" to people like her mother, from whom she is separated "by an invisible wall" (39). Outsiders, "two spectres, wearing childish smiles" (42), the girls develop strategies that manipulate family and social contacts and hasten their exposure to new, ever-stranger sensational experiences. For the narrator such experiences are transformative, almost alchemical. When she desires to attend a fair at night, she says, "I could not explain that when it was dark a new dignity would transform the fair into an oasis of excitement, so that it became a place of mystery and delight" (49). In her quest for such enchantment she hopes to enliven the dull world that surrounds her, albeit through perverse means.

Bainbridge's anatomy of the dynamic between the girls reveals a characteristic struggle for dominance, though the truth of their relationship's shape is complicated by the narrator's unreliable perceptions about it. At times she portrays herself as an obedient pupil of Harriet, for instance, and as her loyal amanuensis. Earlier in her recollection the narrator states that she will not attend art school and explains: "It was Harriet who drew well, not me. It was Harriet who was educated; she told me what to read, explained to me the things I read, told me what painters I should admire and why. I listened, I did as she said, but I did not feel much interest, at least on my own, only when she was directing me" (22). The narrator also claims, "[Harriet] it was who always decided our actions" (54) and "My mind could flood with dreams against fighting against stupidity and evil, but it was Harriet who would realize them" (63). Similarly the words in the narrator's diary are dictated by Harriet (31), though the process had been collaborative until those final days before the end of their summer vacation: "Always before we had both discussed things to go in the diary, analyzed emotions, looked in the dictionary for suitable words, and fashioned the paragraphs sentence by sentence" (32). As their adventures become increasingly complicated and the narrator initiates her own enterprises, tensions over leadership develop between the girls; the unconditional love the narrator professes for Harriet finds its limits. The narrator's boredom and sense of being emotionally deadened, moreover, originate solely within her psyche.

The narrator's other significant social contact is Peter Biggs, whom the girls have nicknamed the Tsar (after abandoning their first choice, Peter the Great). Her relationship with him is ambivalent; although she sees him as "feeble" (15) and mouthing "conventional platitudes" (13), he is also exotic and mysterious because he is an adult male whose friendship with her breaches the decorum represented by her parents and community. Once Harriet returns from a family trip to Wales, Biggs and his wife become objects of fascination for the girls; the man's sexual interest in the narrator and hostile dismissal of Harriet as possessing an evil mind (86) incite the girls to plot schemes that will punish or expose him. In an unconventional way, the girls' plans of action are a means to define themselves and to define the boundaries of their morality.

The Tsar himself is a grotesque and pathetic figure of decay. Self-pitying about his unhappy marriage, his secretive befriending of the narrator reflects his need for a sympathetic and uncritical audience and an alternate source of sexual gratification. Eschewing any simple schema that equates adulthood with predation and criminal culpability and youth with asexual innocence, Bainbridge asserts the unsavory motivations of both. Though the narrator has discerned the Tsar's affection for her—

and so has considered his potential as an experience—it is his sexual kiss at the fair (the nighttime "place of mystery and delight" [49] she had been excited about experiencing) that encourages the girls to pursue their experimenting on him. Later, when the girls spy on the Biggs at their home one night, they see the "monstrous flesh" of Mrs. Biggs atop the Tsar, who sat "pinned like a moth on the sofa, bony knees splitting the air, thighs splayed out to take her terrible weight" (62). Likening Mrs. Biggs to an oiled snake poisoning her mate slowly, the narrator is appalled. She drops her notebook at the Biggs property; and once Mr. Biggs returns it with no admonishment, she decides, "I love Mr. Biggs" (71). Discussing the situation with Harriet, the narrator voices uncertainty about making the Tsar an experience to be written about in their diary, but they decide he is a victim and likes to be punished (72). Again, though conflicted about her loyalty, the narrator sees her love for Harriet as a force that propels her into activity.

Harriet's plan is devoted to enabling the narrator to get over her love of the Tsar. Locked in a church with him, the narrator is contented when she recalls her performance with him, an act that further entangles and disables him: "I had lied very well and cried effortlessly; I would look white and ill in the morning. I thought of the beautiful night and my god-like strength in the church and I began to smile when I remembered the Tsar's banged nose under the lamp. Harriet could not have managed better" (97). Harriet's penultimate strategy leads to the girls being invited to Mr. Biggs's house while his wife is away visiting her sister (who has given birth to a supposedly "monstrous" child [83]) and his married but predatory friend Mr. Hind visits. The men intend to seduce the girls and have little idea that the girls hope to entrap them in some way. While sipping the whiskey served by Mr. Hind, the narrator listens to Mr. Biggs lament the "injustices of old age" and the torment of his unwanted marriage, concluding, "How like a bad poem he sounded" (114). Despite Mr. Biggs being "far too old, far too sad to be helped or turned into an experience" (115), the narrator resignedly accepts his clumsy attempts at intercourse once Harriet and Mr. Hind have left the room. As his tears mix with declarations of love, his silent partner is "memorising positions so nothing should be lost" (116) when she tells Harriet. The narrator, whose unexpected naïveté is shown by her not knowing what "pregnant" means (132), strives to become what Harriet expects while also dedicating herself to defining her individual interests.

Intent on humbling the Tsar, the narrator hands planning over to Harriet: "And at last I gave in to Harriet, finally and without reservation. I wanted the Tsar to be humiliated, to cower sideways with his bird's head held stiffly in pain and fear, so that I might finish what I had begun, return to school forgetting the summer, and think only of the next holidays that might be as they had always been" (130). She arranges to meet up with Mr. Biggs near the beach one evening. His poring forth of "poison and evil" (132) eventually culminates in "raptureless" sexual intercourse, likened to "a visit to the doctor, nothing more" (135). She acknowledges she had been "violated" (139) but also notes "her surprise at how little discomfort she felt and how cheerful she felt" (136) and recalls words that Perjer had uttered earlier in the day: "We all come to it" (138). In depicting the narrator rejoicing in her youth and power, Bainbridge frames heterosexual relations as power rivalries.

The girls reconfirm their friendship and their adherence to their philosophy of experience by returning one final time to the

Tsar's home. The man is drunk and appears to be "thrusting life away from him with all his power" (142). This last visit is chaotic; the narrator decides that Harriet no longer controls the events playing out. She expects disorder and violence to erupt as Harriet and the Tsar engage in a strange battle for power. When the Tsar leaves to obtain cigarettes, the narrator reveals to Harriet that she has humbled him by her sexual intercourse earlier. Harriet is appalled: "Why do a thing like that? We're not ready. You had no right" (148). At that moment Mrs. Biggs returns. Harriet hands the narrator a walking stick and instructs her to hit the woman. The woman is killed, though the narrator believes she did not hit her hard and is, moreover, thankful for being seen by the Tsar because she momentarily believes that her misbehavior will be punished: "I should be punished and purged" (149). An instant later Harriet declares, "We'll say we saw the Tsar hit Mrs. Biggs" (151). The narrator agrees and decides, "I would do whatever Harriet wanted. I would never doubt her again but acknowledge she was more beautiful than me" (151). Harriet erases their fingerprints from the room and instructs the Tsar in the importance of his accepting her version of events, and the girls return home, their screams in the field soon to fill the night.

The scene marks the culmination of the girls' philosophy of sensate experience and, further, their removal from the morality of their befuddled and dull if normative parents. Yet rather than holding the girls aloft in order to scrutinize their criminal amorality (and seeking out its origins), Bainbridge's depiction makes them fascinating; that quality is juxtaposed to and measured against the ordinary and convention-minded profiles of the narrator's parents and sibling. The intensity of the girls' desires and experiences stands in marked contrast to the bland personality traits—oblivious, uncurious, complacent, and sheep-ish—of their families. Although they may be "repulsive almost beyond belief," as the anonymous editor who read and rejected the manuscript of *Harriet Said* claimed, in the textual world Bainbridge has created around them they are relatively attractive because their self-fashioning and intellectual enterprises demonstrate creativity and individuality, albeit of an admittedly perverse kind. Revulsion, after all, requires an accepted notion of normal, good, and right, and in *Harriet Said* the embodiments of those humanistic values are background figures, their sentiments hardly pointed to as valorized and championed norms to adhere to. Lastly, through a disdainful depiction of the Tsar (an immoral and irresponsible adult but, of greater significance, also an uncreative, uncommitted, and weak one), Bainbridge directs an indictment at one character, effectively punishing the figure for his failing by forcing him to take responsibility for the girls' crime.

Though perceived as a chilling "horror story" in the Poe, Lovecraft, and Hitchcock vein when it was published, the realism of the story relates it closely to *A Weekend with Claude* and *Another Part of the Wood*. Bainbridge hallmarks such as banal family dramas, quarrelsome and competitive social interactions, and self-absorbed and intermittently cruel characters, all set amid a landscape that is remarkable for its lack of beauty, are clearly evident in *Harriet Said*.

CHAPTER 3

Perilous Aspirations

The Dressmaker and *The Bottle Factory Outing*

I've never been drawn to the feminist movement. I was
brought up to believe that men had little to do with the
home or children—except to bring in the money. I've
never been put down by a man, unless I deserved it, and
I have never felt inferior. It seems to me that a mutually
beneficial relationship between a man and woman requires the man to be dominant. A sensible woman will
allow the man to think he is the most important.

Beryl Bainbridge, *Paris Review,*
Winter 2000

Compared to the outlandish characterization and hostile
ambiance of *A Weekend with Claude, Another Part of the
Wood*, and *Harriet Said*, Bainbridge's two subsequent Booker
Prize–nominated novels are rooted, as Bradbury noted, in realism, examining close (even claustrophobic) domestic relationships whose apparent ordinariness is revealed to be nonetheless
a repository of desperation, barely disguised fury, unexpressed
regret, and, ultimately, homicidal passions. Even though the
autobiographical novels *The Dressmaker* (1973) and *The Bottle
Factory Outing* (1974) are set in working-class districts in, respectively, Liverpool and London and focus on adult romance
and relationships, they share important commonalities with her
earlier fiction.[1] Both novels feature frenzied acts of violence,

look below the surface cohesion of ostensibly close-knit and functional social groupings, and portray disagreeable and even morally reprehensible characters whose hallmarks are their vanity, selfishness, and cruelty. In *The Dressmaker* Bainbridge depicts the clash of values between two sisters who are raising their teenaged niece in Liverpool. A black comedy that concludes with the corpse of one of its protagonists being stuffed in a barrel en route to Spain, *The Bottle Factory Outing* is also a close examination of the psychology of heterosexual women whose sense of completion and fulfillment is intimately tied to romance and marriage.

Bringing Up Baby: *The Dressmaker*

The decayed and disfigured world occasionally remarked upon by the narrator of *Harriet Said* is depicted with great visibility in *The Dressmaker* (1973). The pervasive atmosphere of havoc, deprivation, and destitution caused by World War II affects the characters insofar as the tried and true (and supposedly timeless) values of tradition have been brought into question and the years of self-denial have fostered a sense that such ascetic repression may inevitably result in a breach. In this bleak setting Bainbridge's anatomy of family relations dramatizes an unending rivalry and conflict between an orderly and self-disciplined Apollonian worldview and a sensual and unrestrained Dionysian one.[2] Passed from one generation to the next, the value conflict produces no victors and no reparative insight: instead of undergoing transformation or learning to modify their perspective to make their circumstances more livable, characters embodying the values exhibit instead an entrenched incapability. In keeping with O'Neill's delineation of entropic comedy, Bainbridge's novel both expresses a loss of certainty about enduring truths and maintains a narrative distance, observing and mocking rather than offering prescriptive or ameliorative plot trajectories. The reviews expressed praise, albeit with caveats. The *Times Literary Supplement* noted that the "grim little tale" with a "cruelly bare" story was a "remarkable achievement," emphasizing that Bainbridge's "imagination pushes her towards nightmare, and her eye for detail is macabre." Although Karl Miller in the *New York Review of Books* called it a "magnificent book" about isolation and family strife, the reviewer wondered, "Does she make an entertainment, a performance, out of this true stuff, doing it harm?" In noting that the ending "has a touch of *grand guignol*," the review expressed misgivings about the author's moral imperative. The *Listener* praised the "sinister little tale" (taking especial interest in one character's "puritanical destructiveness") and called Bainbridge "a formidable talent" comfortable with grotesque characters and macabre nastiness. The *New Republic* scrutinized Bainbridge as a writer of "ostensibly psychological thrillers" and concluded that despite her "sure sense of the conflict in her characters between self-knowledge and self-deception, between the person and the role, between the situations and its idealization," the novel was not ultimately satisfying because of an unresolved conflict between her impulses to write works of entertainment and serious novels. The *Atlantic* discussed her depiction of an "almost unbelievably dreary and inhibited English family" and regretted that the "experienced domestic-horror buff will, unfortunately, have foreseen" the conclusion.[3]

Formally *The Dressmaker* is similar to *Harriet Said*. Its first chapter serves to illustrate the denouement and resolution of a momentous event that will soon occur. The novel begins in chapter "0" with the word "Afterwards" (7) and so informs readers that the subsequent ten chapters will culminate in the now undisclosed event. The portent-laden Christmas season scene of "0" depicts a woman who finds a degree of satisfaction in her home's front room, where "everything was ordered, secure" (7); in that room, later likened to the British Museum, the woman expresses relief that her mother could not take umbrage with her since the room's only fault was the result of "war damage, not neglect or carelessness" (7). Scattered glass shards, and statements like "There'd been enough disturbance for one night" (8) and "You're better off without him" (9), hint at a recently transpired episode of domestic dispute and violence.

Chapter "0" also serves to introduce the novel's principal characters. The adults share family ties. Nellie, a puritanical dressmaker, is the head of the household; usually worried about maintaining appearances for neighbors and clients alike, her worshipful fealty to her deceased mother establishes her sense of righteousness. Nellie's "foolish" younger sister Marge, whose eyes burn (like those of the girls in *Harriet Said*) "with the secrets of experience" (8), has sensualist traits that regulatory Nellie closely monitors, following her parents' lead. Since amoral Marge could not "accept what was right and wrong" and has "more feeling than the rest of us" (117), she was regularly beaten when she was young and she insisted on forging her own path. Though their widower brother Jack does not reside in the house with his sisters, he is regularly there because Rita, the daughter he is unable to properly care for, stays with Nellie and Marge. A weak if intermittently bullying man (who recalls Lionel in *Another Part of the Wood*), he sides with Nellie and falls into confused silence when he is asked to express opinions. His ineffectual communication—"The habit of speech was lost to him, he could only talk platitudes" (103)—renders him a toadying figure within the family dynamic.

The final and pivotal character, Rita, is the sole representative of the family's generation of youth. Accordingly, David Punter discusses the novel as "chronicling the grotesque shapes which the passage to maturity might take."[4] Although Rita is "exhausted" and "pale with loss" (9) when she is introduced, her "wingeing" is dismissed by her caregivers as hormonal: "She was at the age for it, but it was trying for all concerned" (8). On the cusp of a sexual awakening, Rita emblematizes her family's future and acts as a catalyst for its sibling rivalry. Building on the hostile and harsh interrelations of *A Weekend with Claude* and *Another Part of the Wood*, Bainbridge introduces characters and relationships that are noteworthy for their seeming lack of love and excess of spite. The connection between the two sisters is, then, less a bond than a stranglehold. And the tension between them is characteristically high: Marge directs outrage, resentment, and hatred at her elder sister, and Nellie replies in kind with "fury" (10). Rita, the focus of their parenting ideas, acts as a conduit through which the sisters air past grievances. Yet despite the extremity of the emotions, both women are shown expressing tender, protective feeling toward Rita.

The first chapter is set four months before "0," in late August. As portrayed by Bainbridge, desultory Liverpool is an apt setting for the grim and unsupportive interactions between the family members. For example, descriptions—of unmarried Nellie's former place of employment, now a cavernous bomb site, of great clumps of weeds, of a sign with "one corner eaten by rust" (15)—complement Rita's uncomfortable stroll with her acquaintance Valerie:

> The overwhelming ripeness and confidence of the older girl caused [Rita] acute embarrassment. Valerie was larger than life, prancing along the pavement with her heavy body

clothed in a green and white frock made by Auntie Nellie, arching her plucked brows, fluttering her eyelashes shiny with Vaseline, opening and closing her moist mouth, the colour of plums. It was the glossiness of her. (14)

The ravaged setting and the generalized "air of decay and obliteration" (78) reinforce the view of war as physically and socially destructive. In addition to war, though, the change in topography is the result of rampant urbanization and industrialization. As Rita recalls, "Once there had been meadows and trees, cows grazing, ducks on a pond—before they claimed the earth and built the wretched little houses: the industrial revolution, Uncle Jack called it, when they took the green and pleasant land and made it into a rubbish dump, with dwellings fit for pigs, the sky black with smoke from factories" (136). The enervation of the landscape in turn deprives its inhabitants of esthetic inspiration and respite. In fact Bainbridge's narration implies that it actively encourages their sense of forlorn hopelessness and alienation.

The material scarcity and deprivation of Liverpool—from rationing and clothing coupons to black market foodstuffs—affect all their lives and appear to reflect the pettiness and squalor of the household, a house (presided over by the devout character of their deceased mother) that seethes with anxiety, regret, envy, and lack of forgiveness. The household's principal tension is a historical one between two sisters. Nellie, who "knew about death" (24) and makes herself "ill with ungovernable rage over a trivial incident" (50), feels that she has been responsible for mending her sister's ways and keeping her respectable for too long. The widowed Nellie is the authority figure of the house, and her sanctimoniousness, which makes her brother Jack feel as though he is in church (26), stems from a close adherence to her mother's rules and her highly developed sense of propriety. Bainbridge emblematically depicts Nellie poised with her scissors, as though she is ever vigilant to snip out all acts of recklessness and carelessness in her vicinity. Dressmaking is accordingly important—"It was the security the dressmaking gave her—the feeling that she knew something, that she was skilled, handling her materials with knowledge; she wasn't a flibbitigibbet like some she could mention" (27–28)—because her knowledge and skill grant her ultimate control over something that is fundamentally shapeless and fluid. By contrast her voluptuous sister Marge, a conscripted munitions factory worker, is carnal and sensual, and she bridles against conventional abstemiousness. From the perspectives of Nellie and Jack, furthermore, Marge is notorious for lacking foresight, common sense, and dutifulness.

In the opening chapters Bainbridge establishes the pattern of their interactions. Although the quarrelsome, selfish, and often cruel conversations recall those between the characters of *A Weekend with Claude* and *Another Part of the Wood*, the sisters' conflicts—about past events, about everyday decisions, about rearing Rita—are in addition indicative of a clash of values or principles, Marge's id-driven sensuality, frivolity, and individualism clashing with austere Nellie's self-denying and ascetic communalism. The engagement during their evening meal is typical. Over dinner Nellie and Marge squabble and insult each other: gloomy Marge stirs her tea "savagely" while Nellie becomes aggressive when affronted by her sister's words (18); they stare at each other with hostility; Nellie stiffens in disgust at her sister's words and exclaims, "You're so common, Marge. The factory has coarsened you beyond belief" and "You're a foolish girl. I thank God, mother has been spared from seeing the way

you've turned out" (19); and Marge grows giddy with indigna-
tion, tells an off-color tale, and then, "having gone as far as she
dared, contented herself with a mocking grin worn for the benefit of Nellie, tears of amusement at the corners of her glittering
eyes" (19). Young, optimistic, and as yet undiminished by the
limitations set by the world and culture, the third person at the
table, Rita, has a neutrality that offers insight into character
motivation:

> It was alright for Auntie Nellie to live grimly through each
> day, doing the washing, trying to find enough nourishment
> to give them, sewing her dresses—she was only marking
> time for the singing to come in the next world and her
> reunion with Mother. It was different for Marge, a foolish
> girl of fifty years of age; she needed to come home, now,
> and find somebody waited. (19)

As *The Dressmaker*'s plot proceeds toward its December crisis, antipathy between the sisters escalates. A day trip in Jack's
car, for instance, results in an intense quarrel, the tone of which,
Jack notes, is unexceptional: "Jack tried to keep out of it. In a
way it was easy, for he had heard of it all before, not the same
subject but the bitterness lying beneath the words" (63). Jack
drives as the "voices went on around him, Marge attacking, Nellie defending" (63). As they goad each other with memories of
the past, accusing each other of sabotage and being the source of
myriad failures and humiliations, and spit at each other "like
cats, arching their necks and clawing at the leather seating of the
car" (64), the uncontrolled fury reaches such a point that Nellie
faints from it. Even recovered, she cannot help but immediately
think with disapproval of Marge's "slatternly ways" (66). The
epic, seemingly eternal, and irreparable battle of wills and ideologies has its basis in the sisters' shared history, and its future is

focused on their surrogate daughter. In fact the polarized perspectives of the sisters affect the atmosphere in which they raise of their ward, not least because in her father's view Rita is an aggregate of their personalities:

> And she did favour the aunts in appearance. She was in their mould—nothing of the dead wife that he could see: like Marge in feature, with a mouth so pale that the upper lip seemed outlined on brown pencil, making it prominent, and with Marge's slightly frantic eyes, startled, owing to the width between brow and lid. But she was Nellie's creation. It was as if the dressmaker had cut out a pattern and pinned it exactly, placed it under the sewing machine and sewing it straight as a die, over and over, so that there was no chance of a gap in the seams. (25)

And it is seventeen-year-old Rita's induction to the world of adult socializing—taking the form of an invitation to a party and to meeting with American soldiers, "so privileged, so foreign" (28), "riff-raff" (31) whose wealth of food, equipment, and cash inspires envy and disdain—that propels *The Dressmaker* to its violent conclusion.

Rita's miserable acculturation into adulthood is focused in particular on a troubled romance with Ira, an American soldier. When she attends the party, she is separated from Marge, her chaperone, and pairs up with the soldier, onto whom she quickly projects a blissful marital future in the United States. Yet the subsequent furtive romance between Rita and Ira is desultory; its success is doubtful from inception. For Rita, furthermore, it is often humiliating and disillusioning. Raised on a diet of Hollywood romances and yet aware that she does not have the "knack of conversation" because "all her life she had been used to being spoken to without the need to respond" (43), Rita is confounded by romance, exhilarated one moment and crushed the next. If extremes of high and low are conventional attributes of infatuation, Bainbridge's depiction is that much more exorbitant. Though Rita grows "so anxious for the love story to begin" (45) and sees in Ira someone "like a movie star, larger than life" (46), she is also aware of how far from the mark their love story falls. During their walk in the countryside, for example, they pass scarred streets, factories, camouflaged depots and goods yards, warehouses, and bomb sites. They see "the dog dirt on the floor and the human excrement and the soiled pieces of newspaper" (55). This moment and others like it contrast with Rita's Hollywood ideal: "On the films she had seen women wandering down deserted country roads, dappled by sunshine, about to meet lovers or strangers, and they all swayed with a particular motion of the hips, as if they were bare under their clothes. She herself moved stiffly, she felt, like a nailed up box" (45). Such is her need for love and romance, however, that when Ira offers her a "small lenient smile" she is "instantly restored, untroubled" (54). This bipolar pattern of extreme emotions—the "pain of being with him was almost as dreadful as living without him" (96), as Rita thinks—that occurs during her first "search for love" (69) repeats throughout its duration, Rita herself coming to realize that "if there had been less space in her life before his coming, he would not have taken up so much room" (109). Yet once possession blazes up in her, she is consumed by the fact that "someone belonged to her" (56–57).

Through Marge's involvement with and evaluation of that same party and her ambivalent feelings about Rita's subsequent courtship, Bainbridge highlights the conflict between social duty and self-satisfaction. Marge regards the party as wanton, but that judgment cannot be separated from her perception of being an outsider and a failure. Among the vibrant young people, she silently admonishes the excessive use of coal and the laxity of morals: "There was a war on, of course, and she knew attitudes were different, but there was such a thing as a responsibility. It would serve Mrs. Manders right if she became the proud grandmother of a bouncing piccaninny" (32). She later comments that the war "had made everyone lax, openly immodest" (37). As an uninvited chaperon, however, she feels "superfluous" (30). Seeing everyone enjoy the festive atmosphere, she begins to grow introspective, pitying the failure of her life to be at all remarkable. She complains that she was "never in the limelight" and that she "never felt . . . that people took enough notice" (35). Rita's developing romance fully awakens Marge's partially dormant quest for personal fulfillment and revives memories of the injustices she experienced in her youth. Her earlier romance with an unsuitable man named Mr. Aveyard had been brutally quashed by Nellie and Jack, and her own questioning of their mother's parenting skills and their effects is met with outrage and incredulity. She regards herself as a "casualty" (85) of her mother. Yet her wondering whether "all them rules, going to church" (82), and other restrictions caused damage is rebuffed by Jack, who is outraged by his sister's "daft" perspective (82). The influence of their deceased mother—remembered by Nellie as a sainted, model Christian and by Marge as an oppressive matriarch—underlies the chasm between the two sisters as well. And though Marge had earlier lamented the changes wrought by war, she openly challenges the values of her mother and Nellie, of "being proper" at the expense of self-expression. When she says, "It's the war. People aren't the same. That sort of person isn't needed anymore. The past is gone," Jack is shocked and infuriated at hearing his sister and mother being "relegated to the scrap heap" (83). Despite the frequent clashes, Bainbridge indicates no progression; the family members retain their rage, fear, and set points of view from beginning to end.

In her conflicted relationship with Rita, Marge envisions finding both a way to redress her past woes and a vehicle through which to explore vicariously pleasures long denied her. Yet Bainbridge is emphatic about her inability to achieve these ends; social restrictions and individual limitations effectively mark transformative efforts as futile. Marge is entranced by the promise of the city, suddenly "turned into Babel, the clubs and halls filled with foreigners" (98); even so, she reports Rita's secret courtship to Nellie and Jack because it places her in a good light and makes her seem responsible and right thinking. This right thinking relates to her forbidden romance during Rita's childhood when her siblings, convinced that women of her age became possessed of "foolish notions" (40), compelled her to end the nascent affair. Marge also views her niece as a competitor who will hinder an opportunity that rightfully belongs to her; Rita in turn feels jealous of her aunt when Ira pays her overt attention. Marge, increasingly marked by "certain indications of hysteria" and "lack of judgment" (79) according to Mrs. Manders, behaves erratically because she is unable to resolve her internal conflict.

The family's subsequent formal meeting with Rita's suitor is miserable for all the participants. Bainbridge's attentiveness to miscommunication and antagonism renders the scene blackly comic. Moody Rita, who has come to feel anger and revulsion for her aunts (93) and exasperation with and disdain for her father (who has in the meantime decided that he has "nourished a viper in his bosom" [107] despite his best efforts), does not comprehend the odd behavior of her family, Ira, or herself.

Marge, meanwhile, studies Ira. Though she knows that she is
not sophisticated, Marge nonetheless knows "what sort of man"
Ira is: "empty inside," "incurious," "washed clean of subterfuge
and apology" (110), "untouched by schooling," and "ungodly"
(111). She twice tells Nellie, "He's no good" (112). Nellie notes
that Ira does not take his eyes off her sister (whose very pallor
irritates Nellie because it gives her the air of a tragedy queen
[113]). Xenophobic Jack, lastly, regards his daughter's suitor as
"a product of mongrels, the blood of every nation in the world
mingling in his veins—nothing aristocratic, nothing pure" (113).
The meeting is made tenser by Rita's anxiety about the attention
that illiterate Ira directs at Marge and her own erratic emotions
that veer between daydreams of marriage and despair about her
shortcomings. Jack considers warning Rita about love (which he
considers a "virus in the blood. A perpetual state of fever" [133])
but tells Marge that such an attempt would be fruitless: "She
wasn't of an age. She wouldn't understand that love was mostly
habit later on and escape at the beginning" (118). When Rita,
humiliated by her family, her own waspish behavior, and Ira's
inattention, begs him to make another trip to the country, he
makes a vague promise to call. Although the inability to maintain mental composure or to communicate effectively might be a
situation to lament and analyze, Bainbridge's depiction of it
highlights the grotesquerie of the characters and their circumstance. The tableau, in short, has satirical dimensions; the excessive qualities limit any sympathetic or empathetic response and
instead encourage a distant and derisive one.

The final chapters depict the household as possessing even
greater tension than usual. Rita alternates between Hollywood
daydreams and "sitting on the sofa with a face like death" (124),
whereas Marge is sullen and withdrawn, formulating a plan of

action. The coming winter and the gloomy habitat induce Marge to join the Dramatics Society, which needs performers for its Christmas pantomime. Feigning illness the day of her audition and at home alone, Marge is scandalized but excited when Ira appears. After he complains of Rita's lack of vibrancy, Marge excuses herself to go to work and bitterly regrets her weak "uselessness" (129), understanding that men are attracted to her glittering facade, a thing they simultaneously regard as disposable. Her conflict—in contrast with Nellie, who having been "too busy nursing mother to experience that kind of thing" (130) is left cold by Rita's anguish—pits her own satisfaction against her sense of responsibility. For the moment, she decides against viewing Rita as an obstacle to pleasure with Ira: "The malice drained out of her. It wasn't competition—it was little Rita, without a mother and father. . . . Jack and Nellie had moulded Rita, cramped her development, as surely if they had copied the Chinese, binding the feet of infants to keep them small" (131).

The novel closes with Nellie working on the final fitting of Valerie Manders's dress. She ponders the futility of feminine rebellion (145) while immersed in the beauty of the dress, its film star glamour buoying her spirit. When she returns home, she discovers Ira there, buttoning his trousers. She hears a noise and expresses outrage at his offense: "How dare he scratch Mother's furniture. A lifetime of sacrifice, of detailed care" (146). Angered to action—"She was that annoyed" (146)—Nellie stabs him in the neck with her scissors. After he dies, she decides that "she had done wrong" but that "mitigating circumstances" (147) absolved her of actual guilt. Although Marge speaks of wickedness, Nellie's declaration, "We haven't done much in the way of proving we're alive. I don't see why we should pay for him" (148), and their mutual fear of neighborhood gossip encourage them to collude. Nellie, "a dressmaker to her bones" (149), sews together a bag into which they slide Ira; Nellie persuades Jack to dispose of the body in the nearby river. The return to family unity and surface calm—"[Nellie] stood there for all the world as if she was taking the air" (152) before she begins polishing the sideboard in the front room—leaves them only with an obligation to offer so-lace to Rita, whose disreputable American suitor has apparently skipped town.

The normalcy Bainbridge indicates in "0" also signals the failure of character and community transformation or growth and the relative success of the stalemated conflict embodied by Marge and Nellie. Bainbridge's portrayal makes it easy to envision the characters bickering and expressing their regrets and ire until their geriatric years, never once having learned to change their circumstances. Any reader expecting psychological development or a refiguring of communal mores that might be based on an understanding of the liberal humanist novel will be confounded. Although Krystyna Stamirowska notes that the novel's "tension is often resolved by black comedy," the ability of such a comic perspective to achieve resolution is uncertain.[5] Ultimately each sister remains locked within her view and is unaffected by the perspective of the other and even unable or unwilling to understand it. The termination of Rita's romance, finally, suggests the uninterrupted continuance of a multigenerational pattern.

Careerists: *The Bottle Factory Outing*

As with *A Weekend with Claude* and *Another Part of the Wood*, in *The Bottle Factory Outing* (1974) Bainbridge traces the miscommunication and thwarted aspirations of a small, ostensibly close-knit group gathered for a brief recreational idyll. Like those earlier novels, too, the idyll is anything but pleasant; weather, landscape, and human folly conspire to ensure that the event is miserable, if ultimately revelatory. And in keeping with the focus of *The Dressmaker*, Bainbridge's Booker Prize–nominated and Guardian Prize–winning novel pays particularly attention to the interrelations between two female characters with disparate personalities. Although the novel features great fractiousness and a murder, it is more jovial than *The Dressmaker* and decidedly comical. The tension between the characters is characteristically extreme and the novel closes with the unplanned (and possibly accidental) killing of one of the central characters during the factory workers' social outing, but Bainbridge's emphasis on the surreal absurdity of both the characters and their various situations encourages the sort of mirthful response that farce aims to induce.[6] The literary prize nominations were matched by worthwhile reviews. The *Times Literary Supplement* reviewer judged Bainbridge to be a "fine and invigorating writer," albeit not perfect: "The outrageousness of the black comedy, the flirtation with spookiness and the bizarre makes this a less controlled novel than *The Dressmaker*, and one which, though good, is not without its awkwardnesses." Peter Ackroyd, the *Spectator* reviewer, noted that Bainbridge "sets her face resolutely toward the sad and the seedy, the squalid and the sloppy, and yet she never aspires to cheap sentiment." He stated that "all the elements of comedy are here" but drew attention to the novel's weak conclusion. The *New York Times Book Review* expressed greater praise: "Miss Bainbridge has her comic eye on cultural confusion. She makes us see that it goes deeper than we think and touches more widely than we had imagined." Likewise, the *New Republic* called the "firmly controlled, funny and frightening tale" a "wry comic novel of poses

and play-acting" that is also a quest with scenes of "deftly written travesty." Beneath the comic travesty the reviewer also
detected a serious contemplation of existence: "Daily reality
seems to be a ludicrous game all agree to play, while far beneath
the surface the obscure rumblings of life and death continue,
careless and inescapable."[7]

The plot, typical of Bainbridge's fiction, is minimal and
episodic. After a series of comic mishaps, some of the ethnically
disparate employees of a wine-bottling factory arrive at what
they expect will be a pastoral destination. Once there the two
protagonists, Freda and Brenda, engage in tense or stilted conversations with different male employees. When Freda is isolated
and out of sight in the parkland following the group's communal meal, she is killed (the novel does not resolve whether she is
murdered or a victim of manslaughter). Pretending that Freda
has passed out after overindulging in wine, Brenda and a few of
the other workers return her body to the factory in London,
where they eventually decide to pack it into in a wooden brandy
barrel destined for Santander, Spain. They inform the other
employees that Freda has fled to Spain, the fiction of her impetuous and spontaneous journeying raising no suspicion. They
return to their daily routines.

Bainbridge's immediate focus in *The Bottle Factory Outing* is
the complicated relationship between two English women working in a factory otherwise staffed by Italian immigrants.[8] The
power dynamics and sexual politics between the women and the
group of Italian men who are their colleagues in the wine-bottling facility becomes a secondary focal point once the farcical
events at the picnic outing begin. Similar to Nellie and Marge in
The Dressmaker, the central characters of *The Bottle Factory
Outing* are unaligned by commonalities (excepting their sex) and

polarized in their perspectives. Instead of sharing a family bond and history, though, Freda and Brenda share a rental suite and one bed—a line of books placed between them to preserve the appearance of propriety—in a rooming house and a place of employment. Trapped in and by their circumstances, the women nonetheless strive to fulfill the idiosyncratic compulsions of their individual personalities and to assert the preeminent value of their beliefs, the latter quality leading to interrelations that are frequently—and characteristic for Bainbridge's fiction—combative and hostile.

Since the titular October picnic outing does not begin until the novel's midpoint, Bainbridge's initial chapters delineate the histories and interactions of Freda and Brenda. In keeping with her past literary endeavors, Bainbridge emphasizes their differences and the constant clashing of their personalities and traits. A vibrant and manic sensualist who recalls Marge in *The Dressmaker*, Lily in *A Weekend with Claude*, May in *Another Part of the Wood*, and the narrator of *Harriet Said*, Freda is also a frustrated figure whose various strategies for improving her social standing have not resulted in the desired riches. Bainbridge depicts her as hectoring, self-important, vain, cruel, and yet sad and pathetic. For Freda the outing with work colleagues is worthwhile because it is there that she envisions seducing Vittorio, whom she (akin to Rita in *The Dressmaker*) fantasizes to be a wealthy, sophisticated, and socially established man who will transport her from her current benighted circumstances to the sort of luxury and ease to which a woman like her is entitled. Brenda stands in marked contrast to Freda. Obsequious and easily overwhelmed by the needs and demands of others and perpetually eager to maintain appearances (Brenda would rather "have died than let the other occupants of the house know she used the toilet" [24–25], the narrator explains) and blend in to the point of invisibility, Brenda's plight stems from others taking advantage of her passivity. She might be defined by her common refrain, "I don't want any fuss."

Bainbridge establishes their set differences and antagonism by opening *The Bottle Factory Outing* with a depiction of a hearse passing by the women's flat while they are preparing for a day at the factory. Bainbridge also introduces the farcical comedy in that scene; that current of acerbic humor runs throughout the novel. As the hearse passes, Freda cries dramatically over the death of a stranger, but she is enjoying the moment. In contrast, "easily embarrassed" Brenda avoids looking out the window because she might be seen "gawping" (7) by neighbors. Their exaggerated characters and responses foreshadow the ensuing social complications, each situation worsened by their individual tendencies and flaws. Freda, eager for raw experience and longing "to be flung into the midst of chaos" (9), believes like the narrator of *Harriet Said* that only through extraordinary esthetic experiences does life become meaningful. Besides being responsible for organizing the outing, Freda freely dispenses advice to her roommate: "You are too cut off from life" (8), she tells Brenda with a self-congratulatory expertise, imploring her to participate in social occasions. Brenda's defensive reticence and decorum are a disappointment to Freda because her friend's "lack of control, her passion" (9) had been the quality that initially attracted her. Brenda, coming "from such a respectable background" had impressed Freda because she had walked away from her drunken "brute of a husband" and her "obviously deranged" mother-in-law (9). Hoping to induce change in "born victim" (28) Brenda and to broaden her outlook, Freda, who had all her life "cherished the hope that one day she would become part of a community, a family" (11), repeatedly corrals Brenda into situations and conversation that she believes will hasten those improvements. Bainbridge's narration offers a snapshot image of the fundamental schism between the unlikable pair: "At night when they prepared for bed Freda removed all her clothes and lay like a great fretful baby, majestically dimpled and curved. Brenda wore her pajamas and her underwear and a tweed coat— that was the difference between them" (11–12).

Beyond illustrating the interpersonal jockeying between the women, Bainbridge's ties their behavior to femininity and sexual politics, in particular to that of heterosexual women in the workforce who are ultimately reliant on men and marriage for material security and social stature. For instance, Freda's face grows "distorted with fury at the weather" (8) because she has conceived of herself as being desperately in love with Vittorio and requires a locale for mutual consummation. With her elaborately made-up face, dramatic entrances, and incessant and dramatic speaking at work, she regards the "close and isolated" immigrant workers as "peasants, dulled by poverty" (16) and "beasts of the field" (17) and looks to the owners as vehicles for her social betterment. Her flatmate, meanwhile, is accosted at work even though she expresses no interest in romance or courtship. The unwanted sexual attention from a co-worker named Rossi illustrates Brenda's "extraordinary capacity for remaining passive while being put upon" (23), a result, the narration reveals, of her upbringing: "And if she was offered another piece of cake and she wanted it she was obliged to refuse out of politeness. And if she didn't want it she had to say yes, even if it choked her" (23). If the novel's scrutiny of sexual politics appears to suggest analysis influenced by feminism, its comic resolve to mock the women's characters as well as their circumstances would undermine its putative feminist critique. Without evident sympathy or empathy for the characters, Bainbridge's narration becomes satiric. In framing the women and their poor choices and moral weakness as ridiculous, Bainbridge encourages the derisive laughter that is characteristic of black comedy—in this case drawing attention to a would-be feminist situation but veering away from a feminist commitment to analyze, critique, ameliorate, or remedy it.

Despite the somber backdrop of a looming energy crisis, animals screaming from the nearby zoo, and encroaching poverty (31), the novel's tone is mirthful, mocking, and irreverent and not notably despairing. A miscommunication—the first of many resulting from a language barrier between the Italian men and English women—about that morning's funeral procession leads to the pair being granted a day off to mourn the death of Freda's mother (her mother actually having died when Freda was a teenager). Freda, feigning mourning for a few days, stays home from work, secure in the knowledge that liquor from the factory will be satisfactory compensation for her lost wages. She asks Brenda to steal a few bottles. For Brenda the workplace is an unnerving terrain of sexual predation; she imagines that alcohol fumes are responsible for keeping the men in "a constant state of lust" (32). Complaining fatalistically to Patrick, whom Freda dismisses as "that lout from the bogs of Tipperary" (34), that "everything breaks" (33), Brenda inadvertently invites him to her house. And as Freda spends miserable time alone off work, she becomes enlivened by the arrival of a letter from her beloved Vittorio that declares his wish to stop by to express his condolences about the death of her mother. Dreaming of "something more," feeling "refined out of existence by the sameness and regularity of each day," and murmuring, "I am not Brenda—I do want something" (36), Freda plots to enrapture her imagined suitor, her thoughts directed to questions of how she ought to appear and behave to best accomplish her goal as well as, shockingly, to ripping Brenda to shreds. "It was power of a kind that she was after" (37), the narration explains, and that power relates to Freda being able to exert control over others.

The unplanned, coinciding arrivals of Patrick and Vittorio result in yet more farcical misunderstandings. In comedy-of-manners style, meek Brenda hides in one part of the house with Patrick in order to preserve Freda's privacy, while Freda's planned seduction of Vittorio is undermined by her drunken mania and erratic movements, both of which frighten him. The unwelcome arrival of Mrs. Haddon, Brenda's estranged husband's mother, with gun in hand, completes the evening's failure. Freda reiterates her belief that Brenda is a victim who requires help (51). For days afterward Freda is "not herself," her habitual rage outbursts now followed by long periods of silence. Her frustration is directed at her inability to enact a role that can transform her social standing, and her anger focuses on Brenda, whose accommodating femininity and colorless passivity make her unexpectedly and enviably attractive to men. With her thoughts turned to the upcoming outing, Freda feels "the beginnings of restoration" (56), her dream of marital success marred only by an "unexpected setback" a day later when her visit to Vittorio's office underscores her distance from her goal. Like immature Rita in *The Dressmaker*, Freda frequently dreams with an "insatiable thirst for all the joy and glory of the good times to come, [and] the life she was soon to know" (61).

The idealized outing, however, begins with comic failure: the expected transport vans do not arrive, giving the assembled workers no means with which to reach their destination. They use cramped cars as the substitute, leaving Freda "white-faced and utterly demoralized" and Brenda saying, "I wish I could die" (67). With Brenda's nervous laughter followed by Freda's mocking laughter, Rossi drives away from London, having "no idea where he was heading" (71). The women quarrel, Freda telling Brenda, "You make me sick, you do" and "I don't blame your mother-in-law trying to do you in. Never saying a word out of place" (71). Vittorio interrupts, physically wrestling with Freda in the car; Brenda winks at Aldo, the driver, to assure him that the entire scene "was only a joke" (72). The incipient violence and intense conflict of the scene would be suggestive of a despairing vision of humanity except that Bainbridge's treatment highlights both the farcical plot and ludicrous characterization. Subsequently the site for their picnic disappoints Freda: "It wasn't as she had imagined. There were no lush valleys or rising hills saddled with yellow gorse. The land stretched flat and monotonous to the edge of the horizon" (74). Yet her flagging spirits are revived upon seeing a castle. Its grandeur, "redolent with History" (75), she says pompously, will provide lyricism for her planned romantic interlude with Vittorio. The groups are soon separated.

Repeating an earlier pattern, Brenda feigns illness in order to allow Freda privacy with Vittorio inside the castle (whose closed off areas and fusty antiquity confound and depress Freda). Alone with Freda, Vittorio complains that she emasculates him (82) and that he already has other marital commitments (83). Like Rita in *The Dressmaker*, Freda hears only the part necessary for her happiness: "She had not heard the concluding words of his sentence. She had heard him say that he could not be less than true to her, and all else was drowned and deafened in the flood of joy that filled her heart and suffused her face with colour. He did love her. He could only be true to her" (83). That instant lasts "perhaps thirty seconds" before being demolished by Patrick, who believes that Freda has assaulted Brenda. Confrontation results in Freda, "filled with hatred" (85), being physically restrained by Patrick as Vittorio, "a coward but terrorized by [Freda's] loud voice" (85), leaves the room. On a parapet with Rossi, meanwhile, Brenda endures his sexual attentions while wishing that her mother-in-law had actually "put an end to this aimless business of living through each day" (87) for her. Recalling Orton, the novel's farcical sexual antics and chronic misunderstandings seem sensible in a comic world unmarked by compassion and self-knowing.

Instead of anatomizing the nature of the characters' situations, Bainbridge's plotting leads toward greater complication and entanglements. The shared meal a short time later is fraught with additional tension. Like a "matron," bullying Freda calls Vittorio a fool and, watching him eat, becomes "repelled by his unabashed vulgarity, the common way he wiped his hands on the grass" (89). The other immigrant men remain monosyllabic and bashful in front of Brenda and Freda. Brenda continues to regret her attendance. A proposed game of hide-and-seek results in Freda's being struck on the cheek by a pebble thrown by an invisible assailant; Freda's thoughts direct more ire and jealousy toward Brenda. Offered a ride on a horse after that incident, Freda imagines herself as Catherine of Russia only to be told by Vittorio that she bounced "up and down like a bag of potatoes" (98). Since Bainbridge is emphatic about the characters' partial perception and overall lack of empathy, it follows that the conflict between them does not diminish. Instead each clash complicates the next. Brenda, for instance, asserts herself with Rossi by threatening to tell Freda about his behavior, and Freda is enraged by Brenda involving her; as her anger grows she is reminded of Patrick in the castle and becomes more furious still and tells Brenda, "Your teeth . . . are terribly yellow. You should try cleaning them some time" (103). Brenda responds with a hatred that frightens her because it reminds her of her mother's "moods of violence" (104) when she was a child.

Drowsy after eating, Brenda naps. She wakes up, sees Patrick with a newly scratched cheek, and after a brief search locates Freda—dead and with a face that "burned with eternal anger" (110). She observes, "Freda's face, splintered into a thousand smiles and grimaces of rage, leapt at her from every leaf dripping under the onslaught of the rain" (110). A mordant comedy of accusation and suspicion ensues. As though to reflect the change of mood, Bainbridge describes the setting with terms both ominous and threatening: "At the squalid ditch another batch of flamingoes pecked at the bank and teetered on Belsen legs over the mud. They looked obscene, as if they bled all over" (122); caged primates scream in rage. Secretly judging Patrick to be the murderer, Brenda now notices that though having strength of character, Patrick is as commandeering as Freda. Patrick, believing that Brenda has the kind of temperament that stops her from being truthful, distrusts their alliance and Brenda's loyalty. Brenda believes that the men blame Patrick for the murder.

Driving with Freda's corpse in the car, Brenda, echoing Nellie in *The Dressmaker*, announces, "What we've done is very wrong" (126). The group seems indifferent, however, each member distrusting the other and striving to escape the situation, eschewing responsibility or even involvement to the degree that it is possible. At the factory, devout Maria, who admired Freda's larger-than-life persona, wails, "It's God's work" (141) and decides that they must prepare her body with respect. Brenda tells one of her housemates that Freda, who "had been saving for years to go to the Continent," has made an impromptu decision to go abroad because "she could do with a break after her mother dying like that" (143). After overwrought Brenda falls asleep, "her face on the table amidst a pile of sandwiches" (146), she awakes refreshed having dreamed of Freda: "Gone was the worry and the fear, the underlying resentment. Freda would have been the first to agree, it didn't matter how she had died—it wasn't any use getting all worked up about it now. Life was full of red tape, rules and formalities, papers to be signed. Hadn't Freda always been the first to decry the regimentation of the masses?" (146–47). Wedged into a hogshead barrel (that is marked as defective), and soaked with "just a little" brandy, Freda is sent abroad; the brandy, Rossi jokes, now has more body than expected. Brenda's last act of rationalizing the crime —"It was the sort of thing that could happen to anyone, if they were tall and they were grabbed in the bushes by a small man. It certainly wasn't anything you could hang someone for" (157)— is followed by a rebuffed call to her estranged husband and a return to a regular work schedule the next day when Freda's barrel is loaded on a lorry en route to the docks.

In contrast to the intermittent black comedy of *The Dressmaker*, *The Bottle Factory Outing* shades a similar portrait of clashing values in consistently farcical tones. The ludicrous characters and situations—what Stamirowska calls "the prevailing of the grotesque over the potentially serious"—encourage a laughter that comes in response to the fundamentally critical and mocking attitude of the author.[9] Hence although the subject matter—relations between the sexes, interpersonal conflict, and homicide—could be considered serious and worthy of sober scrutiny, Bainbridge renders it comical. Accordingly it is possible to discern that Brenda's complacent acceptance of circumstances and her exceptional passivity during her encounters with aggressive or manipulative men suggest that her ostensible victory is less that of an individual's values than that of the cultural status quo. In fact, as Punter notes, Brenda's epiphany only reveals how "there is nothing to be done about fate."[10] Yet the frantic and farcical comedy of the novel discourages a reading of its goal as being a pensive and serious consideration of these clashing principles. Because Bainbridge's characters are ridiculous and largely unsympathetic, they become figures of mirth, and the importance of their social circumstance is likewise diminished.

CHAPTER 4

Domestic Lives

Sweet William, *A Quiet Life*, and *Injury Time*

> A mistake, of course, just as it's a mistake to think that
> the past can ever be scuttled and forgotten. For a while,
> perhaps, we may succeed in submerging those memories
> and influences of lost and bygone days, until, jolted by a
> fragment of a melody, a view glimpsed from a speeding
> train, some words scribbled in the margin of a book, they
> will rise unbidden to the surface, bringing up the past
> with such insistence that we may well choke on it.
>
> Beryl Bainbridge, *Forever England*

The benevolent, festive aspects of the comic genre include the
pleasurable levity and regenerative resolutions of romantic comedy. Although Bainbridge's fiction reflects understanding of these
popular elements of comedy, in *Sweet William* (1975), *A Quiet
Life* (1976), and *Injury Time* (1977) her use of comic structures
and motifs induces laughter without offering notable hopefulness about humanity.[1] Nor does Bainbridge represent social
change or nod to the conventional recuperative conclusion;
instead, entrenched (bad) behavior and stasis are normative.
Typically, then, these comic novels are often disdainful and
scathing: appalling and intermittently reprehensible characters
caught in awkward, uncomfortable, or violent situations encourage shocked response, moments of amused schadenfreude (because unfortunate events are raining on unlikable characters),

and delight with the ludicrous farcical plot. From *A Weekend with Claude* to *The Dressmaker,* Bainbridge's realistic portrayals of family, friendship, and romantic attachments are emphatic in their foregrounding of antagonism, strife, miscommunication, and selfishness; the continuance of those portraits in exaggerated comedic form highlights an ongoing and wide-ranging satiric perspective about human folly, albeit localized in England. And though her refusal to embrace what Rayner identifies as the affirmative and utopian aspects inherent to the broad comic form is suggestive of misanthropy and pessimism, the comic impetus to mock or ridicule also suggests the impulse to correct or repair (if only minimally so). Reviewing *A Quiet Life* in the *London Times,* Peter Tinniswood provided an exceptional encapsulation of her approach: "The ingredients of the Bainbridge landscape are all there—teetering breakdowns, exotic failures, spectacular indiscretions, long slow broodings, riotous excesses."[2] This "landscape" of excess, particularly evident in the novels of the late 1970s, reveals Bainbridge's seemingly amused scornfulness for women, men, and their society; and with its darkly comic contours, moreover, it implicitly draws attention to a perspective whose marked entropic criticality contains scant indicators of betterment or repair.

Love and Marriage: *Sweet William*

Throughout Bainbridge's novels there is a consistent—and arguably misanthropic—critique of the capacity of individuals (though in particular women) for self-deception, especially in the search for love and marital partnership. Coupled with that perspective is another that conceives of individuals as being adversely affected by social forces and their own history and yet often incapable of overcoming or circumventing those very adversities. These elements in Bainbridge's fiction are conjoined in *Sweet William* (1975), a black comedy in which infatuation, erotic attachment, romantic relationships, and love—the latter akin to a viral infection, a "perpetual state of fever" as Uncle Jack in *The Dressmaker* describes it (133)—are simultaneously bane and savior that characters rely on to repair the tatters of their lives and selfhood. The novel's titular charming male is a cipher and a kind of catalytic agent through which a number of interrelated women imagine they find a perfect lover who will transform them or grant them a reprieve from life's hurtfulness and inadequacy. William, a Lothario figure, finds sexual appeal in virtually every woman as well as narcissistic affirmation of his own beauty. Bainbridge does not focus great attention on William's motivations or psychology. Instead she examines the responses of the protagonist, Ann, whose self-conscious 1970s sexual liberation ethos and relationship modishness is tested by William's inconstancy, alternating subtle and blatant deceitfulness, and refusal to be restrained by the desires of anyone except himself. Well received, the novel did attract some negative criticism. For instance, Frank Kermode in the *New York Review of Books* complimented Bainbridge as being one the best writers in England but called *Sweet William* "a shade less impressive than her earlier work." He highlighted the "accurately depressing dialogue" and the portrayal of "deprived and exploited women" as well as the novelist's overall area of focus: "But our lives are distorted like the feet of Chinese women, forever, and all Bainbridge's women are evidence of whatever it was that ruined England and made it absurdly small." Though the *Listener* praised the "frightening and funny" characters, the reviewer also expressed reserve about elements of Bainbridge's characterization: "I never quite believed in William, but Ann is a convincingly comic version of the unliberated women striving for acceptance in a permissive world." The qualified *Times Literary Supplement* review emphasized that the novel, a "funny and observant" examination of "myopia and narrowness," is "not Beryl Bainbridge's best book, but it's probably the sunniest." Katha Pollitt, writing for the *New York Times Book Review*, called *Sweet William* a "disquieting" novel that was "witty and perhaps even more subtly and ominously grotesque" than *The Bottle Factory Outing*. She viewed it as "a strange, sly novel with a great deal to say about the mixture of resentment and dependency often mistaken for love" and "never less than sharply and savagely ironic."[3]

Consistent with her earlier novels, in *Sweet William* Bainbridge's loose, episodic plot traces the action and thoughts of a small group of interconnected individuals over a relatively brief period of time. It is characteristic too that the ostensible beauty of the initial situation—a woman falling in love at long last with an ostensibly caring, generous, and whimsical man—steadily erodes, revealing truths that are in opposition to the expectation the image has initially encouraged. In short order Ann has met William and rejected her previous stodgy boyfriend's engagement proposal. Yet after she becomes William's lover, she gradually learns of his wives, his philandering, and his profound limitations as a romantic partner. And like Rita, Lily, Freda, and Brenda—those Bainbridge characters confounded or destroyed by love—Ann's response to each freshly revealed stratum of William is erratic, manic, and contradictory, her avowal of true and eternal love quickly followed by raging refusals of his character, and so forth. Her eventual pregnancy (and delivery of their male child, which coincides with the last of William's unexplained absences), like Brenda's resigned acceptance of men's unwanted sexual attention in *The Bottle Factory Outing*, suggests her hapless bewilderment at life's fundamental absurdity. Her breaking away from the conventional mores embodied by her mother, moreover, results in a degree of freedom as well as great loss.

The opening chapter establishes another familiar Bainbridge trope: two individuals pitted against each other. In particular *Sweet William* depicts Mrs. Walton having recently visited her daughter Ann, who is engaged to Gerald. Ann recalls that tense visit, having recently wished her mother farewell at the airport. More tradition minded than her daughter, Mrs. Walton, a social climber, offers a merciless condemnation of Ann, who has recently met Gerald, a university lecturer "with splendid prospects" (6), and allowed him to take a posting in the United States without her in tow. When Ann, who before picking up her mother at the airport feels "a little frightened at the thought of facing" her mother (6), asserts her modernity ("We're not living in the middle ages" [9], she states) and youthful disavowal of conventionality, her mother accuses her daughter of being foolish, out of control, and disgusting—"nothing but a prostitute" (10) who has premarital sex. This monstrous figure threatens to leave. Tired and sad, Ann collapses, tears in her eyes. Mrs. Kershaw, the manager of Ann's lodging house, interrupts their emotional scene, later telling Ann that women like the two of them inhabit a world different from the ordinary one of Mrs. Walton. Ann's unspoken response is telling:

> Ann felt it was funny that anyone should call Mrs. Walton ordinary. It wasn't an adequate word. She thought of her mother's piano playing, her scheming, her ability to read French, the strength of her convictions, the inflexibility of her dreadful will. The way she advised Ann to wear make-up—

"Exploit yourself more," she was given to say; "paint your face." As if Ann were a Red Indian. The way she referred to men as "persons." Her use of the possessive pronoun. The subjectivity of her every thought. (13)

Ann had fled the environment of her oppressive upbringing and can only manage a brief imaginary visit to the past: "She could bear it for a moment—the torment of being related to her mother and father, the wounding" (27). Her historical relationship and recent contretemps with her mother influence her subsequent choices about her entanglement with William.

Though she imagines herself as not being "the sort of girl who allowed herself to be picked up by strange men" (17), Ann nonetheless responds to the beckoning of one such stranger, the Scottish playwright William McClusky, at the airport. Flattered by his kind words and intrigued by his apparent nontraditional manner and eccentricity, she talks with him, revealing her irritation with her cousin Pamela's mannerisms, and is then surprised by the malice in her voice and the unworthy, boring, vulgar, and stupid sentiments pouring from her mouth. Ann wants "to be good" (19) though, so, like Brenda in *The Bottle Factory Outing,* she routinely lies and stifles her actual sentiments in order to conform to normative expectations. William's wooing of Ann takes the form of gifts (an expensive television and a silver ring, for instance) and a kind of romantic attention that makes Gerald's seem paltry and undesirable. Ann's sense of iconoclastic, freethinking modernity, however, is soon challenged by William's waywardness and by the fact that he is married and has children.

Bainbridge alternates scenes that offer insight to Ann's character with ones that illustrate manic interactions between Ann, Pamela, Mrs. Kershaw, and William. Ann is a characteristic

Bainbridge figure insofar as she is conflicted and contradictory, veering among hopefulness, cynicism, and despair about parents, day-to-day life, and existence itself ("all that expanse of flesh touched by the grave" she thinks when she sees an "obscene" woman in a bathing suit who provides a stark contrast to William, "beautiful, outlined in light that seemed to waver and coalesce" [32]). She views love—which she likens to a remarkable force that can revivify and transform her, revealing that "all that had happened to her before, in the past, when she had been like herself, had been a mistake" (35)—and William's love specifically as the very element that will eradicate a self that is little other than a defensive response to her upbringing; love, she imagines, will replace that outmoded and undesirable vestige with something adult, full, and mature. Though this transformative expectation suggests the possibility of betterment, it is held by characters in earlier Bainbridge novels and ultimately exposed as illusory or untenable. Still hopeful, Ann vows to prevent anything or anyone from destroying her bond with William, even though she acknowledges the cheaply overwrought nature of her emotions:

> "Aye," Ann said carefully. "He's my man." It sounded a little melodramatic, and she hoped Pamela wouldn't remember the musical that both had seen in Brighton. There had been a heroine who, on hearing her lover singing in the distances—something about the morning mist being on the heather—had cried aloud "My Man" and bounded like a deer into the wings. (38–39)

Despite her initial ecstasy, Ann's continued exposure to William gives her abundant evidence to conclude that he is a habitual teller of half-truths and outright lies; he is vague, noncommittal, and evasive. He eventually speaks of Sheila, his ex-wife, for instance, but neglects to mention till much later Edna, his current wife. Though Ann believes in his sincerity and in love's power of sublime transportation, she notes his distance, that his mind goes on maneuvers that exclude her, and that she "had been happier when he indicated love, not practiced it" (43). She strives to ignore her suspicions and suppress her jealousy of William's intimate friendship with Gus and his frequent tenderness with Pamela, who physically suffers after an illegal abortion. Ann fears William, she acknowledges, and her thoughts dwell on her "insipid and valueless" childhood and her mother's rearing of her: "[Ann] had been taught that men were different; she had digested the fact of their inferiority along with her banana sandwiches and her milk" (46). Ann is confounded by William's reasonableness and his dispassionate explanations for his eccentric traits. Of his past marriages, for instance, he tells her, "It has nothing to do with now" (51), and he dismisses her anxieties by saying, "You've lived a bit of a fantasy life, I imagine. . . . You haven't learned to face things for what they are" (52). She accepts his view but finds herself increasingly skeptical as his inconsistencies multiply. In seeming mockery of the would-be emancipatory politics of the sexual revolution and Ann's self-conscious modernity, Bainbridge heightens the farcical aspect of the novel's plot: Ann's romantic idyll is made yet more complicated and ridiculous by the arrival of the "graceful and a bit silly" Edna, William's wife, whom Ann concludes is "very civilised" or else "simple-minded" (53).

Ann's conflicted needs for a real (as opposed to merely conventional) romantic relationship, to be modern and tolerant (rather than jealous and territorial), and her desire to assert her independence from the thinking and sentiments of her despised mother's generation are intensified as she encounters additional evidence of William's complicated relationships and deceit.[4] She alternates between being compliant and submissive, seeing every event as illustrative of their uniquely intense love, and finding the improbability of William's actions suspicious and worrisome, such as when he tells her after partaking in an anti-Semitic conversation that he is a cipher, "anything anyone wanted him to be" (63). Pamela's return from Brighton, necessitating a trip to the hospital to heal the abortion injuries, prompts Ann's epiphany:

> How far we have travelled, thought Ann, though it was not the distance to the hospital she was contemplating, but more specifically her attitude to life, her abandonment of standards. In ten days she had encouraged adultery, committed a breach of promise, given up her job, abetted an abortion. She had not been aware, throughout these happenings, of any unease or distress. She had become like one of those insect specimens under glass, sucked dry of her old internal organs, pumped full and firm with an unknown preservative. She was transfixed by William. (67)

Thus transfixed, she sees in all of William's actions indications of his intense love for her. Bainbridge's mockery of Ann's blindness is intensified and extended as the plot progresses. Within hours, Ann has learned of another of William's manifold deceptions; she returns to thinking of her mother's assessment of men as "self-absorbed and secretive" brutes (73) and fears that her hands will strike him when he approaches. Despite resenting his constantly forcing her to "make adjustments," she agrees to a plan to go away with Pamela. Subsequently finding William naked in bed with Pamela, Ann confronts her cousin, making it clear that she wants Pamela to leave. Pamela's response— "You don't want to expect normality from him. He's an artist, after all" (80)—implies that she too has been affected by William's charm.

Although Ann's first thought about the cessation of menstruation is that she shares a commonality with malnourished women in concentration camps, William informs her that she is pregnant. In keeping with her own tendency of undermining of conventional expectations relating to genre and trope, Bainbridge does not associate the pregnancy with fruitful regeneration and communal continuance. It is a harbinger without positive connotations. Placed, moreover, in relation to further revelations about character flaws and reprisals, it becomes one comic complication among many. Near that time, for instance, Pamela recants her former adoration of William. When Ann says, "Somebody has to lead" in explanation of the modishness of her relationship with William, Pamela replies, "That's rubbish. Everybody's doing the same thing. You're not leading anybody. You're following" (84). Ann's uncertainty escalates. William's disappearances to unknown destinations increase, yet he thoughtfully buys her family expensive gifts. Outside of William's protective aura at her family home for another miserable Christmas, Ann feels further adrift, possessing "no roots, no continuity" (97). The strain of her realizing that she possesses her mother's vampire instincts and father's reticence (101) and her mother's constant fault finding—in short order her mother says, "You foolish girl," "You disgust me," "There's something radically wrong with you," and "Go to hell" (103–5)—pushes Ann into a feverish state. She returns home to find "a body, two bodies lying on the bed" (106) in the dark, imagining it is Pamela and William. William tells her it is only Mrs. Kershaw checking a damp spot on the ceiling. His lie is obvious, but of necessity Ann accepts the words as truth. As delineated by Bainbridge,

Ann increasingly appears to be victimized. Even so, in highlighting her willed blindness, smug attitude, and ethical vacillations, Bainbridge encourages an ambivalent if not actively derisive response to her.

Once William begins living with Ann, first asserting his dominance by stowing away her books to make way for his, the exposure further corrodes their intimacy. Furthermore, when the provincial tour with *The Truth Is a Lie*, William's risible Beckett-like meditation on the differences between generations, is postponed by six weeks, his odd behavior, sudden absences, and bizarre and improbable misadventures exhaust Ann: "She felt nothing at all. She was empty, absent. Blank" (117). Emotionally withdrawn from William while he is touring with the play in Liverpool, she nonetheless yearns for the light of his affection; and after her mother writes a letter expressing her disgust for Ann's "lack of decency" (119), she replies positively to William's imploring telegram to visit. Bainbridge describes the en route landscape in characteristically nonidyllic terms: "How dirty they were, the cows, splattered with dried mud, sullenly munching. What a mess it was, the countryside, fractured and torn, threaded with abandoned canals, tyres floating along the thick green water—caravans, ruined cars, obsolete tractors, bushes ghostly with lime from a kiln ripped out of the ground" (122).

Once in Liverpool, Ann is overwhelmed by the attention William gives her, but she also confused when he tells her he believes her "capacity for deception was as great as his own" (128). Feeling momentarily invigorated because they seem to have returned to "the beginning, before it got spoilt" (128), Ann is soon distraught when she hears new information about William's past and current romantic entanglements. Like a character in William's play, Ann feels lost and hapless: "She felt his wives and herself were citizens of some special country. They knew about the frontiers, the treaties. Anyone else would boggle at the absurdity of the customs, the complexities of the language" (142). Placing her protagonist between a remote, scheming, and judgmental mother and an inconstant, untruthful, and narcissistic lover, Bainbridge suggests the possibility of sympathy toward the conflicts of a liberated woman circa 1975. More often though, the befuddled and weak Ann raises readers' ire over her continued citizenship in the "special country." Placing Ann in context to Bainbridge's antic and farcical plotting, moreover, colors her further as a ridiculous figure.

The novel closes ambiguously, with "dreadful, disheveled and white as chalk" (150) William attempting to reunite with temporarily resolute Ann, physically as well as emotionally. Under William's spell Ann momentarily falls into her former belief that he is "so romantic . . . so beautiful" (152) until she realizes that lies are part of his personality. Made "vast and distorted" by pregnancy (157), Ann eventually gives birth to her son at home, at William's insistence. William disappears with his could-be lover Chuck as Ann ponders the significance of the hair lock William had shown her during their last break up: "She was trying to remember the particular shade of the glossy clump of hair she had flung away on the heath. There must be an answer somewhere. An identification. One had to know the relationship between people. The whole secret of life was there, if only she could be given the clues" (160). Like Brenda in *The Bottle Factory Outing* or the sisters in *The Dressmaker*, Ann faces upheavals in her life that result in unplanned changes in circumstances but not character growth or insight.[5] Bainbridge depicts the world as fundamentally capricious and establishes that Ann's place in it is tenuous and provisional. If comedy is commonly held to be a redemptive or recuperative genre, Bainbridge's farcical variation highlights human fallibility, mocking it and implying as well that it is a chronic, unchanging condition. Incapable of much growth, challenged by communication, manipulated by friends and foes, and embodying divided and conflicted desires all amid mercurial circumstances, Ann is a comic protagonist whose author, steadfast in her rejection of affirmative comedy, refuses her the traditionally benign closure in what Stamirowska calls a "dark deterministic world."[6]

Family Relations: *A Quiet Life*

Discordant relations are a pulse running through Bainbridge's fiction, coursing quietly alongside the principal plot, as in *Harriet Said* and *The Bottle Factory Outing*, or commanding full attention, as with *The Dressmaker*. Bainbridge followed the farcical if mordant comedy of *Sweet William* with *A Quiet Life* (1976), a somber novel that examines the deleterious childhood of middle-aged Alan and Madge, briefly reunited—after fifteen years of separation—following the death of their mother. In the present day of chapter "0," the estranged siblings meet in a café to discuss the dividing of the possessions of their mother. Alan, stodgy and materially comfortable, stands in contrast to wayfaring and eccentric Madge, whom he had spent six months tracking down in France. Her critical regard for family and decorum is evident in her irreverent words. They affect her brother, whose recollections express his lack of sympathy for her sentiments: "Madge hadn't even bothered to turn up at the funeral. Instead she had sent a distasteful letter written on thin toilet paper, from some town in France, suggesting that if they were going to put

Mother in the same grave as Father it might be a waste of time to carve 'Rest in peace' on the tombstone" (7). Always "a great one for discussing emotions" and from her brother's perspective interested only in the past (10), Madge has a distinctly different recollection of their shared history. When she claims that he was the most loved, her brother is perplexed: "'Loved?' he said. He thought she was mixing him up with someone else" (10). This inconsistency of memory elicits Alan's seeming reminiscence over the next eight chapters. Like *A Weekend with Claude*, the disparity of perspective is chronic and suggestive of a fundamental inability to comprehend objective truth or another's point of view. About this tale of rebellion transformed into "political regression," reviews were largely favorable.[7] The *Times Literary Supplement*, for instance, took note of loss of "a teasing element of grand guignol" in her earlier fiction and concluded that the change leads to "complete credibility with, if anything, a gain in intensity." Francis Wyndham also drew attention to the novel's setting, which "seethes with the hidden violence which underlies so much of everyday life," and Bainbridge's technical mastery, which "produces an unnerving effect of immediacy through the sparest selection of detail presented in the simplest prose." Wyndham concluded, "Reading this book, one feels uncomfortably close to the people and places portrayed in it, yet protected from them by her glassy objectivity." The *New York Times Book Review* viewed the novel as one that "works with the sly precision of a trap" and praised the "subtle and protean writer" for her "feat of concealed craft." The reviewer singled out Bainbridge's historical sense, noting that her 1940s are "authentically drab but returning to them in her company is a delight." The *Listener* review was ambiguous, observing that the author had "toned down her usual black comedy to an even shade of grey" and that "book is short on happenings, Beryl Bainbridge having opted for atmosphere this time."[8]

Chapters 1 through 8 present scenes from the family some twenty-five years earlier, when Madge was fifteen. Alan's recollection concludes with the death of their Stalin-admiring socialist father, Joe, a self-deluded, blustering, and foolish tyrant with pathetic claims of heroism (that recall Lionel in *Another Part of the Wood* and Bainbridge's portrayal of her own father) who "could never be on an even keel—he was either elated or depressed; he knew nothing of in between" (98). Their mother, Connie, by contrast, is a woman with aspirations for higher social standing. Madge remarks on the family's home, a product of their mother's "flair for decorating," as being a minefield (14). Completing the portrait, Bainbridge describes the siblings as a study in contrasts: Madge is rebellious—wandering free at night like the narrator in *Harriet Said*—whereas Alan is proud of his ability to suppress his feelings. Characteristically for a Bainbridge novel, the opening scenes establish the entrenched quarrels of the family. The parents appear to dislike each other and to either purposely antagonize or ignore each another; their daughter tells outrageous lies and involves her family in fabricated traumas—such as running into a strange German man who looks like Hitler—that result in tearful outbursts; and Alan merely tries to escape involvement.

The plot, typically episodic, is a series of vignettes that capture overall family dysfunction and individual reactions to it. Fleeing "a silence more brutal than words" (18), Alan visits the youth club, a place where he is popular. Once there he discovers that his sister had been seen earlier in the day talking to a German prisoner. The following day a visit from relatives illustrates again the tension running through the household, the parents exchanging bitter or sarcastic, goading words. The father, a weak and angry man whose fortunes have been spiraling downward for years, clings to what little authority he can (his Air Raid Patrol uniform from the war being a visible emblem) and worries about being emasculated by his household duties. His wife, "disillusioned time without number" (36), takes a certain satisfaction in the wounds she causes during their frequent quarrels. The children also react to the circumstances, Alan retreating and becoming sullen while Madge grows manic, seeking attention with misbehavior and bizarre antics. Each episode aggravates the family members' anxiety and anger. During the relatives' visit, conflict between Alan's father and his grandfather results in violent outbursts and the exchange of hostile words. Alan's Aunt Nora—who during the war had left their home, preferring the bombs to the continual bickering (73)—declares his home "a mad-house" (38) and promptly leaves. As Father storms upstairs to bed, Mother tidies for a moment before hurling a vase of daffodils into the blazing fireplace (39).

Alan's recollection amply illustrates his family's quarrelsome nature. His father and mother's clashes over money, power, and responsibilities seem to have been running for decades, and the battles between parents and children and between the two siblings have a history as well. Alan, the elder by a few years, is baffled and embarrassed by his sister's wildness—such as her nocturnal wanderings in the woods, a place of undetected mines and unexploded shells—but not because he has any particular fondness or concern for her. Instead he wants to "hammer sense into her with his bare fists" because she does not comprehend how her antics affect *him*: "She didn't seem to grasp that it was the trouble that she caused him personally that was his main concern. He was long past marshalling the reasons for his parents' behaviour—it would be like emptying a cupful of ants into a butterfly net for safe keeping. All he wanted was for Madge to stay indoors at night, so he needn't return to find his father jumping up and down, demented, at a kerb" (48–49). Later, accused by his father of stealing money from his mother's dresser drawer, Alan (who is innocent of the crime) spends a day with his father that illustrates their mutual failures of communication and empathy.

The plot's numerous clashes are intensified by an unexpected visit by family acquaintances Mr. Harrison and Captain Sydney, and by Alan's fledgling romance with his classmate Janet Leyland. The former, an "unheard of" breach of decorum, leaves Alan's parents "white-faced and shaken" (52) and later briefly united by their shared schadenfreude about the captain's physical disability; it also provokes Joe's heightened volatility and jealous reactions to the affair he images his wife has begun with one of those visitors. Alan's uncertain navigation of courtship rituals, moreover, intensifies his overall level of anxiety; accordingly his conflict-ridden relationship with his sister and parents grows worse as he measures them in relation to the enviable normalcy of Janet's agreeable family. With Janet, for instance, he tries to explain his complex family politics, and she questions his parents' ability to raise a family, asking whether they are "daft" (71). After he fumbles in his attempt to fondle Janet sexually, he returns home miserable, only to find a buried bag of shoes belonging to Madge. Gathered together momentarily as a "happy family" (77), they close the evening unhappily: the siblings quarrel and Alan slaps Madge's face. Alan is humiliated: "He got told off for his pains. Father leapt downstairs and belted him over the head. He went to bed in disgrace" (79). Handled as darkly farcical in *Sweet William* and *The Bottle Factory Outing*, the aggregating of unfortunate and misery-inducing events in *A Quiet Life* does not induce derisive merriment about the fate of corrupt characters but a horror about the dysfunction and the inability of the characters to change it or themselves.

Bainbridge's plot is constructed around misunderstandings, partial knowledge, failed attempts, and overreactions. As a result the characters appear to be hapless, incapable of meeting socially or self-imposed expectations, and become distraught. Alan, for instance, remains ambivalent about his newly cemented romantic relationship with Janet. He is "not sure that he cared to be taken over so completely" by it and is baffled by Janet's behavior (79), which seems to require responses that he cannot fathom. Even so, he is attracted to her and the normative values she represents, despite the squabbling, pettiness, and chronic miscommunication (similar to the squabbles between Rita and Ira in *The Dressmaker*) that leave Alan equally excited and dismayed. His emotional distress is amplified once he returns home. Reading with a "pretence of detachment" (84), Alan nonetheless feels hatred and disdain for his unhinged father, now enraged and furious about all manner of events, especially his wife's supposed scandalous affair. Janet's subsequent visit to Alan's concludes with Connie showing off her finery while Joe vengefully burns his wife's antique chair outside. Another exchange of threats and bitter words ensues. The next day, while en route to visit Aunt Nora on her birthday, Alan and Madge quarrel loudly. Inside Nora's rented home, that "mean little house with the ugly patterned wallpaper and the curtains stained yellow with age" (96), Alan nods off, only to awaken to his father quarreling with

Nora about his wife's unfair treatment. Alan discovers as well that his father is bankrupt; the day ends with the father silently accusing his wife of infidelity.

Alan's impassive reminiscence of a courtship complicated by his family's theatrics reveals Bainbridge's seriousness as well as her comic perspective. Compared to the Leylands, Alan's family's "barmy" antics (102)—of late, his mother's nightly disappearance, his father's scouring of the neighborhood in search of his absent wife, and wayward Madge's ongoing affair with a German prisoner—verge on the surreal. The final family adventure soon after, a trip to the seaside, is marred by Alan's awkwardness with Janet and his sighting of Madge's sexual foreplay with the German prisoner. He laments and is angered by Madge's abnormality and lack of feminine propriety. When he tells her, "You're too young. It's not right to go with men of that age," she responds, "There's no rules" and asserts that "in years to come, lads like you will take to drink, or aspirins. Mark my words" (135). Another confrontation later reveals the whereabouts of Alan's mother—solitary and reading in the waiting room at the train station. As with perpetually adversarial Dionysian Marge and Apollonian Nellie in *The Dressmaker*, the entrenched position of each family member remains intact, guaranteeing only its miserable continuance. Although Bainbridge's perspective can convey the lamentable harm it causes, comic exaggeration and farcical plot elements frequently render its participants laughably and nearly grotesquely incompetent.

In the last chapter of the novel set in the past, a broken window frame and clock result in a riled-up Father and tearful Mother. Janet's subsequent unannounced visit to Alan's home torments him because she is exposed to the paltriness of his family's possessions and the meanness of his family life; in the presence of Janet, Madge reveals Alan's secrets and that he keeps things bottled up, "anything for a quiet life" (148). Alan realizes that his sister's outspokenness stems from the same desire as his secretiveness: "to avoid embarrassment" (148). Typically, however, the realization does not instigate change or progression. Instead family members remain unchangingly obstinate and quarrelsome. The following day Madge tells her brother that she plans to become the German prisoner's lover. Incensed, Alan lashes out at his father, telling him about his mother's train station respite, to which Father expresses disbelief. Alan, "consumed by malice," tells his father, "You make her sick. You make her flesh creep" (151). Joe, now "prostrate with grief," runs outside and begins to saw down the sycamore tree he had been threatening to cut down for years. The exertion leads to his fatal heart attack. Either relieved or indifferent, Connie throws out the emblematic Air Raid Patrol cap once her husband's body has been removed.

The second chapter "0," which closes the novel, depicts Alan returning homeward after his visit with his estranged sister. Amid the setting of decay—he walks "averting his eyes from the old perambulators and rusted stoves that hooligans had flung over the railings on to the once grassy slopes where the crocuses had bloomed" (155)—Alan thinks of his wife, Joan, and her loneliness. He feels regret for her unsatisfactory family ties: "She'd had an unhappy childhood. She didn't come from a close family, not like him and Madge" (156). In exposing Alan's final sentiments as smug and blatantly self-deceiving, Bainbridge undermines both the credibility of his superiority to Madge and the image of the conventional "quiet life" as indicative of good living. In mocking Alan's conventionality as well as highlighting his misguided certainty, Bainbridge simultaneously reduces him as a sympathetic figure and exposes him as the deluded object of the narration's scrutiny.

Infidelities: *Injury Time*

In her early works, beginning with *A Weekend with Claude*, Bainbridge maintained a consistent focus on small groups gathered in relative isolation—a brief stay at a house in the country, a picnic at a rural park, or a weekend spent at a cabin in the woods. Following the cynical humor and multiple locations of *Sweet William* and similar geographically dispersed depictions of family misery in *A Quiet Life*, Bainbridge returned to scrutinizing bad behavior in close quarters in *Injury Time* (1977), a boisterous farcical novel. As in *The Bottle Factory Outing*, much of *Injury Time*'s plot unfolds during a social gathering: a shared meal. The ordinarily simple event veers absurdly and violently far out of control; instead of revealing any heroism in the dinner party guests, the novel revels in the mayhem, mocking the corrupt relationships, fractured communications, and various failings of community and individual characters. Read as a novel about "false and confused quests"[9] and the sterility of culture,[10] *Injury Time* received generally positive reviews. The *Listener* noted Bainbridge's "customary aplomb and precision" and her "unerring sense of the absurd" but was "not so sure about the precision of her touch at the end." Calling *Injury Time* "extremely funny and very disturbing," the *New York Review of Books* reviewer praised the author ("one of the most distinguished writers now working in England") and her depiction of "a situation that is entirely normal and thoroughly disgraceful." The review highlighted her "undeceived wit," "lightness of touch," "precision of detail," "faint exaggeration," and "splendid irony." In the *New York Times Book Review* Katha Pollitt applauded Bainbridge's "black comedies of Britain's postwar disarray," in which "characters grub for certainties in the ruins of a civilization they can barely understand and which is plainly too much for them: the menace of the commonplace overwhelms them." Pollitt lamented that although *Injury Time* "has moments of comic vigor," it "reads like a trivializing of Mrs. Bainbridge's best work, almost like self-parody."[11]

Bainbridge opens her novel with a picture of harried, middle-aged Edward Freeman, a partner in an accounting firm, fantasizing six hours before a dinner party he plans to attend with the Simpsons. The unlikable, self-pitying protagonist imagines that "a small coronary might do him a world of good" because "he could just lie there for several days, undergoing tests, doing a spot of reading, trying to sort himself out" (2). A call from his wife, Helen, confirms that he habitually claims to work late in order to avoid a mature marriage full of rarely stifled complaint. A second call, from his worldly mistress, Binny Mills, establishes that Edward's illicit relationship is volatile and uneasy. In order to appease Binny's heightened sense of neglect and insignificance, Edward has agreed to begin introducing her to his friends in respectable social situations. Although glum Edward recalls the beginning of their affair with nostalgia and is concerned that promiscuous Binny could be "riddled with disease" (8) and that her insults could turn into violence, the relationship offers him an escape from routine and his overwhelming sense of being the boring occupant of a life devoid of value. When his quarrelsome conversation with Binny concludes, Edward's hands are trembling; through those hands and Edward's anxious belief that it is "vital that nobody drop in" (11) during the dinner party, Bainbridge foreshadows the onslaught of unplanned events that will engulf him.

With the addition of neurotic comic characters, Bainbridge assures plot complications and guarantees that the ameliorative goal of the dinner will not be met. Binny's housecleaning and food preparation, for instance, are interrupted by her friend Alma Waterhouse. Since Binny does not want Alma to know about her dinner party, she throws the vacuum cleaner into the backyard and her dessert apples into a bag that then falls behind her refrigerator. Alcoholic Alma, "a great believer in swiggies" (15) and currently suffering from husband difficulties, shows up with a bottle of whiskey and encourages Binny to step outdoors. There the women encounter a world "menacing and full of alarms" (22) and observe "several elderly men and women drinking out of a communal bottle" sprawled "in disorder across the rusted springs of a double bed" (18). Binny's sense of impending chaos and lack of control are further reflected by her meek thankfulness for not being run down at a pedestrian crossing. Subsequent engagements with Alison, her angry and foulmouthed eighteen-year-old daughter, and an evangelical man who preaches from Luke 15:7—"Who are the just persons who need no repentance?" (51)—intensifies her, and the novel's, sense of disorderliness. As Binny is preparing for her guests, Edward is preparing his colleague Simpson, whose wife Muriel may not react well to dining with a man and his mistress. Bainbridge's setup, so emphatic about miscommunication, looming threats, and anxious worry, makes it plain that the ensuing events are not so much improbable and irrational as they are reflective of unpredictability and vital unknowability within the novel's world.

Bainbridge emphasizes the looming violent chaos of the world as well as the fragility and seeming continuous decay of the Edward and Binny's amorous relationship. Each is filled with unspoken sentiments. Binny, who hopes "they both might feel something, some emotion that would nudge them closer to one another," also wonders why her lover did not "pretend that he longed to leave his wife, so that she in return could pretend she wished he would" (56). Edward, who feels unfairly criticized, ducks in anticipation of a slap when Binny reaches out to touch his cheek. Through their counterparts, the Simpsons, Bainbridge exposes additional marital failings: becoming lost en route to Binny's home they exchange bitter words, Muriel incorrectly assuming that her husband is a puritan incapable of an affair while George is "thinking how unfair it was that the nicer moments of life—a few drinks under the belt, good food, a pretty woman seated opposite—were invariably spent in the company of one's wife" (63–64). Overall the atmosphere is tense with deceit and unexpressed resentment.

Appropriate to farce, conditions steadily erode once the Simpsons arrive. The signs preceding dinner are discouraging: the Simpsons arrive late, Muriel gets annoyed when her husband abruptly leaves (to call his mistress at a pay phone), Simpson injures his leg and damages a spoon, and the dinner itself is overcooked. All the characters drink to excess and enact social performances that are as excessive as they are insincere. Bainbridge shifts focus among members of the quartet but highlights their harsh (and usually inaccurate) evaluations of one another and the constancy of their miscommunication. Uninvited Alma later shows up drunk and disorderly, and the guests have idiosyncratic responses to her comically disheveled appearance. Muriel, for instance, views her as a "child dressed up for a party" (96), though her husband thinks "it was in dubious taste to compare Alma to a child. Granted her eyes and mouth seemed to have been crayoned in by a two-year-old with an unsteady hand, but in every other respect the woman was a tart" (97). As the characters agonize over blows to their egos and pass judgment on fellow dinner guests and Binny's house, Alma vomits violently. After helping Alma clean her clothing, Muriel walks to the front stairs outside the house. She is immediately hurled inside the house by three gunmen and a hostage (who is in fact a member of their gang).

Though the tension of the dinner party pales in comparison to the violence of the gunmen, Bainbridge's depiction of the all-night assault highlights the pettiness of the characters, their wrongheaded assumptions about one another and their situation, and their frequent misunderstandings. Whereas in *A Quiet Life* her narrative's attention to the characters' divisiveness reflects with lamentation on the flaws of humanity, here it becomes comical and ridiculous—those same flaws and the large chasm between noble ideal and petty reality a source of and cause for laughter. Faced with evidence of what Edward labels "decaying society [and the] gradual breaking down of law and order" (122), the dinner party guests—now hostages—squabble and offer divergent opinions about the origin and motivations of the criminals as well as the best course of action. In reply to Edward's "cooperation theory" (129), for example, Simpson proposes a diversion that will allow one of the hostages to break free from the house. Hostage unity is impossible, however: Each man believes the other is foolish and in search of heroic glory. Each man also thinks of how his extramarital affair is having a negative effect on his quotidian existence. The criminals, meanwhile, squabble and then fight violently. Despite the hostages' certainty that the police are using high-tech surveillance on the house and have a plan of rescue, the police do not immediately arrive.

The criminal gang decides that Edward and Simpson are a threat, so the men are tied up with torn bed sheets; Binny experiences shame about her worn sheets, and Edward wets himself and feels humiliated. Binny begins to form what she thinks of as a strategic relationship with a gang member named Ginger—whom newly awakened Alma judges to be weird (158) immediately before talking to the wall, assuming that there are police listening devices recording her every word. Brought together after Muriel shrieks, the group gathers in "the festive atmosphere of the room" (163). Even though he loudly states his moral opposition to Edward's infidelity, Ginger apologizes for making Edward's marital problems worse. Edward, proclaiming that he was glad to be at Binny's side during the ordeal and proud of his "bravery and indiscretion" (163), momentarily feels a surge of love and accomplishment in relation to Binny. Moments later Simpson's failed escape attempt—foiled by the vacuum cleaner Binny tossed into the back yard earlier—ends with a gunshot and changes the convivial atmosphere. The hostages and the gang feel ire at his attempt: "Everyone's sympathy lay with the gunmen" (169). Believing that Ginger will confide in her about the gunmen's plans, Binny is surprised when he instructs her to lie down and remove her stocking in preparation for his sexual assault. Listening to Alma's laughter downstairs, Binny's thoughts turn to her experience:

> She supposed she was being raped. One huge tear gathered in her left eye and rolled down her cheek. She wasn't being hurt or humiliated—he didn't do anything dirty or unusual. He wasn't stubbing cigarettes out on her despised breasts or swinging from the chandelier, member pointed like a dagger. It was unreal, of no account. That's why she cried—though she wondered why it was only in one eye. (177)

She resolves to tell no one because "people would have doubts" (177) about her culpability.

In rendering the hostages preposterously irritable and quarrelsome, Bainbridge subverts expectations typically accorded to the situation: worry about the well-being of the hostages and sympathy for their ordeal. Bainbridge's portrait maintains a steady focus on flaws and inconsistencies. The following morning, for instance, the group's uncomfortable sleep the night before leads to heightened irritability and despair. Edward is described as an "incontinent tramp" who "looked terrible" (181); seeing his "creased and ravaged countenance," Simpson realizes that "his dancing days were over" (182); Binny laments that she is "filthy dirty and worn out" (184) when Edward begins to speak of dedicating himself fully to their relationship, and Alma, "corpse-like in her satin dress," is shown to have "turned to skin and bone in the morning light" (181). Muriel, in contrast, has a "full and rosy" mouth that looks "wholesome" (181). The generally sour mood contributes the growing lack of goodwill among the hostages. The experience, pondered by Simpson, does not encourage the closeness he expected:

> His wife sat a million miles from him, playing with a thread of cotton at the torn hem of her frock. He had always imagined that this sort of experience drew people closer together, made them nobler and more sensitive. He'd seen photographs of survivors of such drama, and it had seemed to him that their eyes were tranquil with communal suffering. (192)

Ordered upstairs to help the ailing female criminal, Muriel tells Binny of a miserable extramarital episode moments before they discover that the female is only a man in disguise. The novel

Domestic Lives / 101

closes with Binny's confiding in Edward about the rape. Edward's strange response—laughter—draws her wrath. When Binny and "too fat" Edward are taken as hostages into the vehicle the bank robbers have obtained from the police, Edward says, "I'll never leave you" (212) to her moments before he is thrown from the fleeing automobile. Binny thinks, "Liar," as a woman witnessing the scene utters a scream.

The inconclusiveness of *Injury Time*—Does Edward die? What happens to the remaining car occupants? How does the hostage taking end?—points to its farcical nature: although amusing, the novel's dedication to listing the unexpected and consistently unfortunate events being faced by characters notable for terrible behavior, slack morality, and unpleasant personalities also foregrounds its critical attitude toward the characters and their various fates as well as its critical remove from them. That distance encourages readers to view those characters with a disdainful glee; they are fated to discontent and misery because, in a sense, it is what they deserve.

CHAPTER 5

Closures and Transitions
Young Adolf, Winter Garden, Watson's Apology,
and *An Awfully Big Adventure*

> There's no point in writing about what everybody knows,
> and I don't want to have any hindsight. I pretend I'm
> there, at the time, like the people I'm writing about, and I
> can't let them know what they wouldn't know.
>
> Beryl Bainbridge, *Publishers Weekly,*
> 9 November 1998

Following the formal comic perfection of *Injury Time*, Bainbridge began to extend the scope and purview of her novels, placing a notorious historical figure into a comically dissolute Liverpool setting in *Young Adolf* (1978), depicting a hapless adulterer's absurd decline while traveling in the Soviet Union in *Winter Garden* (1981), portraying a miserable Victorian marriage that culminates in murder in *Watson's Apology* (1984), and, in *An Awfully Big Adventure* (1989), offering a grimly comic account of an adolescent's immersion into the world of theater and adult romantic complications. During this period of transition Bainbridge also published *English Journey, or The Road to Milton Keynes* (1984), a chronicle of her 1983 travels that followed the path set out in *English Journey*, J. B. Priestley's Depression-era examination of the soul of the nation; a short story collection, *Mum and Mr. Armitage* (1985); and *Forever*

England: North and South (1987), an examination of six geographically dispersed English families that speculates about "the notion that England is two nations."[1]After writing *An Awfully Big Adventure,* Bainbridge has set her subsequent novels, from *The Birthday Boys* (1991) to *According to Queeney* (2001), in remote historical periods.

Hitler in Liverpool: *Young Adolf*

Barbara Millard explains that Bainbridge suffered from writer's block after *Injury Time* and, moreover, agreed with those who believed she ought to write novels with greater scope and avoid further fiction based on her life and childhood.[2] One result of this block was increased involvement with scripts for film and theater, journalism, and public lectures. Another was a tour of Israel with a group of writers that led to her renewed interest in the Holocaust and Hitler. Millard reports that on a later visit to New York City Bainbridge saw an entry in the diary of Bridget Hitler that claimed Adolf had visited her husband Alois in Liverpool in 1912.[3] The resultant mordant comedy, *Young Adolf* (1978),[4] marks the beginning of Bainbridge's progressive focus on historical subjects, subjects that eventually included the Watson murder case of 1871, the *Titanic*, the Crimean War, the Scott expedition, and the final years of Samuel Johnson. The turn to history is no surprise, as Bainbridge's statements—such as "I have never been able to appreciate the present or look to the future" and "I have never been intrigued by the present or curious about the future"—seem to prophesy the eventual purview of her work.[5] How Bainbridge uses the tools of historiography and represents the past, though, is ambiguous and open to interpretation given her stated lack of interest in "hard facts" and suspicions about the politics of historiography:

We rely on the evidence of written history for a knowledge of the past, and generally speaking it is a mistake to do so, for all the great events have been distorted, the important causes concealed, and most of the principal characters who figure on the page have been so misrepresented and misunderstood that the result is a complete mystification. The ordinary man, for the most part, has been left out altogether.[6]

Bainbridge acknowledges, moreover, the necessity of "inclusion and omission" in any portrayal, and suggests the impossibility of total recovery or complete representation: "In every human character and transaction there is a mixture of humility and humbug; a little exaggeration, a little suppression; a judicious shifting of responsibility. The truth for every one of us, whether we be on the screen or in front of it, is always subjective."[7] The differing approaches Bainbridge takes to the historical novel genre in *Young Adolf* and *Watson's Apology* reveal that she has no explicit orthodoxy or template for historical fiction; the comic portraiture and fabulous antic plot of the former is clearly distinct from the empiricist claims of truth, realism, and authenticity in the latter.

Reviews of *Young Adolf* applauded Bainbridge's new direction. The *New York Review of Books* used terms such as "disconcerting," "amazing," "highly original," and "immensely skillful," and it asserted that Bainbridge is a novelist whose preoccupation is the "increasingly bewildered and helpless England." The *Listener* identified the novel as a "delightful fantasy" and a "highly comic book, but one that also has a cutting edge." The *Spectator* commented with approval about Bainbridge's "surreal burlesque" of the "larval dictator," and the *London Review of Books* reviewer saw it as "plain and hilarious sailing," a story "provoking the sort of mirth one experiences after a narrow escape." Diane Johnson, in the *Times Literary Supplement*, likened Bainbridge's novels to a "family of eccentrics" and described *Young Adolf* as "not a historical novel in the usual sense" but "an invention of another kind, a feat of imagination and craft, without definition." She called it impressive because "we are made to sympathize and pity the monster of the world. It is a complicated exercise in social sympathy that Bainbridge demands of us, and is her most ambitious treatment yet of the serious concern and conviction that underlie her comedy."[8]

Young Adolf is unprecedented for Bainbridge insofar as it represents a grafting of her thematic foci—familial and marital discord, ethically compromised and frequently loathsome characters, blackly comic plotting, and a decaying and oppressive setting—to a consideration of a prominent historical figure (*the* towering figure of evil and infamy of the twentieth century, no less). As such the novel must be read in light of Hitler's later doings, as a psychological anatomy of the notorious figure *avant la lettre*. As a travesty of the latter Hitler or even as speculation about the psychology of the eventual führer, Bainbridge's depiction, though sympathetically illuminating a troubled personality, is also characteristically comic, emphasizing young Adolf Hitler's sheer ridiculousness and his unwarranted megalomania. She strips the figure of his vast, almost metaphysical aura of evil: this early Adolf is silly, petty, unstable, and socially handicapped. His latter incarnation bears so little resemblance to her portrait of a bumbling and ranting youth that via it Bainbridge suggests a number of possibilities: he was mad rather than evil, his rise to power was a kind of senseless historical accident, and his country's embrace of him reflected its own madness.[9] Moreover, ever attuned to the adverse effects of her own nation's culture, Bainbridge's depiction of Adolf's ludicrous misadventures on what he comes to call the "lunatic island" are part of the ingredients in the recipe that produces the führer. Yet Bainbridge does not dwell on implications in her novel. A characteristic series of weird episodes and fractious engagements, *Young Adolf* is reflective of Bainbridge's ongoing interest in illuminating the quarrelsome and unfulfilling relations between close-knit individuals in a capricious and not infrequently hostile universe.

Bainbridge begins her portrayal with ambiguity. Young Adolf Hitler, age twenty-three, is en route to his elder brother Alois in Liverpool circa 1912. The pathetic Chaplinesque figure[10]—impoverished, famished, on the run from Austrian military authorities, mentally strained (he is "maddened by doubt" [6] and burdened by the belief that he is being followed by an Austrian spy), literally trod upon, and reading a "wild west" novel by the popular German writer Karl May—bears little resemblance to the fearsome eventual leader of the Third Reich. Bainbridge's portrait aligns him instead with figures such as the Tsar in *Harriet Said*, Lionel in *Another Part of the Wood*, or Brenda in *The Bottle Factory Outing*: individuals ostensibly victimized by life's circumstances and easily overwhelmed by the demands of social interaction. Upon arriving in Liverpool, Adolf is introduced to an unwelcoming home environment. Alois's involvement with his "artist brother" (13), Adolf, and his wife, Bridget, is awkward and unsettling, contributing to the deterioration of the already listing marriage. Bridget's marriage to a "foreigner" (she "had fallen in love instantly, as though struck down by influenza" [10]) had been followed by revelations of his shady and failing business enterprises, a history of crime and incarceration, irresponsibility, and violence. Bainbridge highlights the marital faults, emphatic about Bridget's isolation and Alois's controlling abuse. The harsh Liverpool setting contributes to the already oppressive atmosphere: "In the opposite direction the street sloped endlessly downhill, out of sight, past the rows of blackened dwellings, the Brewery and the Home for Incurables, the Soap Works and the Bovril Factory, and ended at the warehouses and the docks. There wasn't a tree growing on it from here to the river" (23).

Adolf's stay in Liverpool is worsened by his boastful, advice-giving, and dissembling brother, a failed restaurateur-cum-waiter and razor-blade salesman, as well as by his own litany of personality defects. Frequently at odds with his brother about their shared history and perspectives on the world, Adolf himself is anything but a calm and complete individual. Bainbridge showcases him as bewildered, weak, gullible, passive, assailed by doubts, paranoid, dogged by a "sense of failure" (28), angry, hostile, and consumed by regret about the fateful effects of impoverishment. His mood changes are mercurial and suggestive of incipient madness. For instance, when Alois offers his brother a secondhand coat, he witnesses Adolf's "absurd expression of rage" (33) that leads to his snarling like a cornered fox. Alois, "staggered by this rather effeminate display of snickering frenzy" (33), then stands witness to Adolf poised to lash out violently while "ranting incomprehensibly about vermin and redskins and men with beards" (33–34). Bainbridge's Adolf displays a veritable catalog of eccentric antisocial behaviors; pacing, paranoid, sensitive to criticism, obsessive, and enraged, he is characterized as a case study rather than a fully formed individual. Pointedly, speaking with the Jewish Mr. Meyer about race contamination, "bastard peoples" (57), and cultural decadence, Adolf reveals familiar beliefs that will remain with him as a political leader; Bainbridge attributes them to his anger and frustration for his various failings in life ("It's a rotten world" [57]). Moreover, during an outburst directed at his brother, who has recommended that Adolf obtain employment as a waiter, Adolf exposes a secondary psychological root for his numberless troubles:

> "'He was illegitimate and so were you. He married three blasted times. You were beaten so regularly that if you dropped those elegant trousers we'd still see the marks of his belt. . . . He was a bastard. Both of you. Bastards.' And gibbering with loathing [Adolf] ran to the hat-stand and leaping in the air spat a gob of saliva at the photograph [of their father] on the wall" (71–72).

In addition to unsuccessful interactions with family, Adolf has awkward relations with other inhabitants in the rooming house, such as the unkempt Dr. Kephalus, whom he regards as a lunatic and disgusting philosopher. Each day there are incidents that support an understanding of Adolf as suffering from mania. He views seasonal decorations as detestable and revolting because they remind him of his mother's death. His continued encounters with ominous strangers culminate in a visit to a supposedly empty third-floor room that seems imaginary because when he revisits the room no evidence supports his memory of it. A trip to the countryside for Christmas greenery presents Adolf with further opportunity to register disgust at the rotting, leaden, and rubbish-heaped landscape (85). Wandering, he encounters the bandaged man from the third floor. He tells Meyer, "I am perpetually stalked by unknown enemies" (94), telling him he believes they are agents of the Austrian military. After Meyer consoles him by stating that the event has "temporarily affected your natural good sense" (96), he reveals that the bandaged man in the room is a labor activist. Adolf's momentary return to placidity—signaled by his cradling his nephew and judging the snowy landscape to be worthy of a painting by Brueghel—concludes abruptly: he is "disproportionately hurt when Bridget failed to remark that he too was good with children" (98). Shortly after the trip to the countryside, Adolf's Christmas dinner tirade once again showcases his unstable personality. Bainbridge's description conjures the crazed comedy of the scene. Besides the bizarre incoherence of Adolf's speech, his audience's reaction reinforces the scene's surreal quality: Alois speaks of defecation and hemorrhoids, while Bridget strives to understand a small percentage of his accented words and Meyer provides corrections to his inaccuracies. Adolf, speaking of the mystical experience of transcending his puny body (109) and becoming "an airborne creature soaring on iridescent wings above the earth" (109), finishes suddenly: "Then abruptly he sat down. Misjudging the position of the chair he fell to the floor and disappeared under the table" (110). Dr. Kephalus judges him to be hysterical, and the others remain silent.

Bainbridge gradually focuses scenes on Adolf's engagement with the larger world, further illustrating his polarized response from certainty to bewilderment, comfort to awkwardness, confidence to confusion. Beginning work as a room service waiter at the Adelphi Hotel, he feels "in his element" among the opulence and grandeur. In veering from comic characterization to farcical plotting, Bainbridge further emphasizes the lunacy of character and setting, and in doing so she simultaneously mocks Hitler and resituates him, with ambiguous effects. Placing Hitler inside the Adelphi and making deliveries for enigmatic Monsieur Dupont—whose prophetic words to Adolf, "Things are never as they seem" (19), might apply to the novel's plot and the figure of

Hitler himself—Bainbridge's inventiveness revels in comic absurdity. Adolf is ludicrous, and the cast of characters that involves him in secret plots, subterfuge, and political activism is fanciful and improbable, like a screwball, Chaplinesque comedy.[11] Eventually and unwillingly implicated in a complex and bizarre skirmish between labor activists and representatives of the city, and witness to a scene "so melodramatic in content and so jerkily enacted, that he felt he was watching a show at a moving picture house" (133), Adolf grows convinced of both his own importance and the insanity of the world. The novel's finale, involving Adolf attired as a female character from *The Merry Widow* operetta and the mysterious bearded man revealing his belief that Adolf is his son, also results in Adolf resolving to never to be mistaken for a woman again: he decides to grow a mustache and vows to leave the "accursed city and lunatic island" (158) for continental Europe. Although the irony of Meyer's final words, which close the novel—"Such a strong-willed young man. It is a pity he will never amount to anything" (160)—is plain, the fusing of Bainbridge's characteristically derisive and comic elements of the domestic novels with the historical novel's focus on a significant historical figure produces a polymorphic narrative—surreal fantasy, comic misadventure, satiric fish-out-of-water tale, and psychological meditation.

Soviet Absurdity: *Winter Garden*

Although *Winter Garden* (1980) is the first of Bainbridge's novels to be set outside of England,[12] its farcical plotting, fractious social interactions, and steady flow of absurd moments align it with her two previous novels, *Injury Time* and *Young Adolf*. In fact *Winter Garden*—depicting one man's impulsive outing to the Soviet Union (in order to escape from an ordered, dull, and increasingly lifeless marriage) with an exuberant and quixotic, albeit erratic and untruthful, mistress—reflects Bainbridge's steady movement toward a misanthropic dystopia. In particular its situating of vain, obtuse, mercenary, petty, and cruel characters in a setting in which order and patterns are frequently interrupted by absurdity is suggestive of the distressing universe and existence dramatized by Beckett in *Waiting for Godot, Happy Days*, and *Play*. Bainbridge's novel is also in keeping with her previous writings insofar as the ostensible meaning-affirming nature of its genre—in this case both comedy and quest—is undermined and denigrated; both questing hero and quest are rendered as hopeless as they are preposterous.

The novel's reception was positive. The *Spectator* reviewer placed the novel as "a phantasy in which the Kafkaesque strangeness and the Waughian . . . humour reside in the fine structure of Beryl Bainbridge's idiosyncratic prose." The reviewer placed it, moreover, as a transitional work that illustrates Bainbridge's moving away from solid naturalism toward a style "dominated by a vein of anarchic, surreal humour." In the *New York Times Book Review* the novel was described as a "graceful, disturbing thriller" addressing "very major matters," and in doing so, it "leaves one on the tantalizing edge of understanding." Anne Duchene, the reviewer for the *Times Literary Supplement*, noted that the "comedy fails to comfort" and compared Bainbridge in her use of language to Harold Pinter and Stevie Smith. For her, Bainbridge created a unique atmosphere in this novel: "Comedy is secreted everywhere, like honey; but it is a surreal little honeycomb, with sharp teeth." The *Listener* called *Winter Garden* "funny and alarming," a "paranoid comedy, where nothing can be trusted to work, where the routine which used to govern the novel is grotesquely involuted or else suspended." It was viewed as a "creepily jokey thriller" that "frightens and mocks us" into nearly renouncing "the good sense of things."[13]

The counterpoint between protagonist and environment serves as the central structural element of *Winter Garden.* Although Bainbridge uses the "stranger in a strange land" theme that historically has encouraged satire (as in Montesquieu's *Persian Letters*) and cultural examination (Doris Lessing's *Marriages between Zones Three, Four, and Five,* for instance), her portrayal does not encourage reader sympathies because the protagonist's concerns, hardships, and dilemmas are increasingly ridiculous, and moreover, the world that delivers him woe is also ridiculous, though in the manner of the prankster Puck rather than the Ministry of Truth. It is the protagonist's limitations that Bainbridge places in the foreground. The middle-aged lawyer, Douglas Ashburner, shares qualities with any number of Bainbridge characters (such as Marge in *The Dressmaker* or Freda in *The Bottle Factory Outing*); like Edward in *Injury Time* he strives to supplement his banal subsistence with enriching experiences, those beyond the mundane or scantly satisfactory emblematized by his twenty-six years of marriage. In contrast to the aforementioned female characters, however, Ashburner is obsequious and lacking in courage. Unable to abandon the comforting routine of his marriage, he tells his wife that he is taking a fishing trip. In company with his mistress, moreover, he is passive and accommodating. He yearns to break the confines of his "enclosed existence" with a "furtive and inconclusive" affair (94). But because his creative response to the stultifying circumstances of his life also reflects his weakness and cowardice—he cannot envision leaving his wife or changing the direction of his career—his quest becomes punitive, surreal, and wholly beyond his control. This "outing" to a foreign place showcases both the violent absurdity of the world and the inability of an individual (whose moral rectitude has already been introduced as suspect) to exert pattern or control over it. The comedy, such as it is, results from the near-farcical series of events that envelop him and undermine the recuperative goals of his journey; the antic behavior of the feckless comic types he travels with and the ludicrous conditions within "most bureaucracy-ridden country in the world" (122) buttress that dark-hued comedy.

Bainbridge's close attention to Ashburner's traits reveals a contradictory figure. Though guilt ridden and self-justifying, he has never been separated from his wife for more than a day; and yet he remains convinced that he was unlike and superior to her because, he believes, she "lacked any deep awareness of birds, of flowers . . . and those desired flashes of consciousness so essential to development" (9–10). By stressing Ashburner's unwillingness to acknowledge or even see his hypocrisy and flaws and his concomitant eagerness to blame others (his wife, his employer, his father, his childhood), Bainbridge directs the reader's response. What is more, Ashburner's attempts to escape from the banality of his middle-class middle age further establish the failure of his enterprise. For example, although Ashburner's extramarital situation promises psychic respite or amatory revitalization, his younger mistress, Nina, an artistic free spirit famed for her beauty and known to carry herself "like Joan of Arc at the stake" (13), suggests another imprisoning relationship. Married to a brain specialist who is too busy to travel with her as part of a group invited to view art by the Soviet Artists' Union, Nina, with her self-serving behavior, amply illustrates how poorly she will serve as a remedy for Ashburner's ills. Frequent commentary by Enid and Bernard, her acquaintances and artistically inclined colleagues, serves furthermore to demonstrate how completely unsuited the lovers are for each other.

The novel's first six chapters, capturing the departure from London and arrival in Moscow, establish patterns that are characteristic of Bainbridge's fiction. The protagonist's relations with others are erratic, unstable, and uncertain; anxiety, resulting from breaches of etiquette, misunderstandings, antagonistic behaviors, and sudden and unexpected changes of plan, becomes the protagonist's fundamental emotional state. Dislocation and fear result as well from exchanges with their authoritarian and angry hosts; and evidently mistranslated and censored information from Soviet citizens amplifies the tenseness. The novel subsequently follows the tourists as they attempt to find edification and satisfaction amid chronic problems that are exacerbated by the censorious Soviet officials. Despite the profusion of odd events (that escalate, beginning with lost items of apparel) and his heightened sense of confusion, Ashburner consoles himself with the belief that "the next twelve days must be lived with all the fervour of which he had once been capable" before the return to "calamity and penury" at home (33). Led by Olga Fiodorovna, a cipher whose pro-Soviet translation services mark her every utterance as unreliable, the group embarks on the tour, often finding their desire to see "real" artists and artistic expression ignored in favor of state plans to see official art and art collectives. The profusion of unsettling occurrences—a lost hat, missing documentation, waylaid luggage, strange telephone calls—culminates in the disappearance of Nina. Ashburner's fear and worry are tempered by assurances that her disappearance can be logically explained. During her supposedly temporary absence, he relies on the ostensible friendship of Enid and

Bernard, people he generally dislikes and whose opinions and outbursts leave him "bewildered and offended" (70).

To scenes of Ashburner's bafflement and discomfort with his circumstances, Bainbridge contributes others that emphasize the group's nonsensical misadventure. For instance, when Boris Sha-belsky, a comrade of Nina's, takes them for a drunken dinner at an artist's forested estate fifty kilometers from Moscow, Ash-burner is attacked by a three-legged dog. The attack is followed by scenes of rambling, drunken, and confusing conversation in an overheated room during which Ashburner is rendered nearly unconscious by wine. He is sent to have a hot bath to calm his nerves; awaking to find the water cold and the bathroom door locked, he escapes via the window, only to be attacked once again by the vicious dog. Outside his familiar surroundings and faced with improbable and foreboding events, Ashburner's state of mind alternates between feeling "trapped within a monstrous butterfly net" (83) and possessing freedom of will. Bizarre and disconcerting events such as the murder of an artist, Nina's ongoing absence (explanations run that she might be ill, institu-tionalized, kidnaped, or lost), and missing possessions disturb Ashburner; and yet on the eve of a night express train to Lenin-grad, he has a vision of himself overcoming the creativity-crushing and damaging experiences of school:

Now, alone in a foreign country and inexplicably function-ing without the support of either wife or mistress—he hadn't even missed his dog—he began dimly to rediscover that lost boy who, compelled at school to read certain set nov-els by Dostoyevsky, had for a brief twelve months feebly wrestled with the notion of divine punishment and self-punishment. Can it be, he thought, smiling and nodding appreciatively at the metal worker, that Mother Russia is a catalyst? (95)

Ashburner's putative rediscovery is short lived. Yet another unforeseen and disturbing event—being "ravished by a random traveler" (100) while on the train (initially suspecting it may have been Enid or Olga, he later wonders whether the event had been a dream)—is followed by a trip to a massive hospital, where he is mistaken for Nina's brain surgeon husband. Viewing a corpse, he sees a distinctive scar of Nina's and passes out. He wakes up in a hotel only to be reproached by dutiful Olga for misbehavior.

With the escalation of uncertainties and oddities, *Winter Garden*'s mockery of human foolishness changes tone; the increasing intrusiveness of the arbitrary or capricious malevolence of its universe shifts the strict focus from the risible action of characters to setting and circumstance. That said, Bainbridge remains steadfast in her depiction of the antic misadventure of the touring group. During a reluctant and delayed trip to a theater production of *Faust*, Ashburner, preoccupied by events of the preceding days and hostile thoughts about his wife, catches sight of Nina in the audience. When she disappears once again, he suspects that she was being "manipulated by others and was in serious danger" (118). Giddy about the ludicrousness of his situation but placated by his travel companions, Ashburner then informs Bernard, "One or two things are not quite ship-shape" (123); Bernard subsequently explains that he has syphilis, which must be treated with pills that Nina gave to him at the beginning of their trip. The three then fly to the Tblisi district, a locale marked by decay, dishevelment, and fatigue, where they are promised tours of collectives and churches. Taken instead by the president of the Artists' Union (and his two prostitute companions) to watch an obscure allegorical film in an unfinished cinema, Ashburner visits a lavatory whose walls and ceiling are covered with excrement (133). He begins his third day in the Tblisi hotel feeling disoriented, his mind "usually simple, was a confusion of dark and intangible thoughts" (137). Though Enid regards him as insecure and attention seeking, Bainbridge's depiction emphasizes a surreal incoherence—from scenes of drunken sailors to non sequitur conversations about dogs, Rasputin, and English criminal cases. Nothing of value is learned, and little communication occurs without misunderstanding; and the tour—itself based on reason: logical planning, specific destinations on specific dates, goals to reach at each destination—proves to be arbitrarily directed and even nonsensical. That provincial tour concludes with an anxious, hurried, and incomplete trip to Stalin's birthplace. When they travel to a "special monastery in the mountains" (150), Ashburner has what Enid deems a "supernatural revelation" (152), seeing Nina and becoming convinced that she was murdered at the artist's studio where he had been attacked by a dog. Enid and Bernard, considering Ashburner "wracked," turn to ponder instead "how Ashburner had stumbled on the art of loving; love depended on the ability to like oneself and required an understanding of eternal regret" (153).

The return to Moscow is upset by the apparent theft of Ashburner's fishing rod and the appearance of a note in Nina's handwriting. Ashburner concludes he is the "victim of some monstrous conspiracy. He was being used to expiate some misdemeanor, some crime perpetrated against the State" (157). Bainbridge neither confirms nor denies Ashburner's perception and so tacitly approves of his parting sentiment as he awaits his fate in near incarceration in Moscow: "Even the man who is

sensible and composed, he thought, must pale before life's contradictions" (157). The target of laughter as an embodiment of
weak-willed hypocrisy throughout *Winter Garden*, Ashburner's
final moment transforms him into a pathetic figure—and not
only a simple figure of fun—who has been undone by enigmatic
forces with unknown goals. Bainbridge's comic vision conjures
an absurd existence—marked by action without meaning, movement without purpose, communication without understanding,
effort without reward—and does not point to resolutions or
amelioration. Embodying O'Neill's model of entropic comedy as
that which exists in response to the "erosion of certainty," *Winter Garden* describes a world of inexplicable occurrences, miscommunication, and meaningless activity that becomes only
increasingly hostile and incomprehensible by the closing pages.[14]

Murder in the Past Tense: *Watson's Apology*

At first glance *Watson's Apology* (1984) bears little resemblance
to the novels preceding it.[15] It contains none of the farcical comic
plotting, caricature, derisive and mocking humor, and absurdity
of *Winter Garden, Young Adolf,* and *Injury Time*. Moreover,
compared to *Young Adolf*, Bainbridge's first historical novel,
Watson's Apology appears distinct since it adopts the quasi-
documentarian approach of the conventional historical novel
wherein, as delineated by Fleishman, a novelist aligns herself
with the historian as a "recoverer of what actually happened"
through "more or less accurate" description and interpretation
of historical moments.[16] In fact *Watson's Apology*, portraying a
miserable Victorian marriage and the resultant notorious murder
case, begins with an author's note explaining that the novel
is based on an actual case, and that although the "documents
presented have been edited here and there to fit the needs of the

narrative," they are otherwise authentic. Bainbridge adds: "What has defeated historical inquiry has been the motives of the characters, their conversations, their feelings. These it has been the task of the novelist to supply" (6). With mention of authenticity and truth, then, as well as an affirmation of a close relationship to historical inquiry, the novelist confirms an allegiance to the realist recovery strategies of classical historical fiction. Furthermore, unlike Linda Hutcheon's postmodern historiographic metafiction, a genre of historical fiction thought to interrogate the political ideology of historical narratives and consciously draw attention to the limits of representation, Bainbridge is explicit in her acceptance of historical fiction's ability to adequately represent moments and sentiments lost to historical inquiry. Despite its innovations and distinctiveness, however, the distraught and cruel characters, oppressive setting, and disturbingly hostile social intercourse portrayed in *Watson's Apology* are familiar because they are characteristic elements throughout the decades of Bainbridge's fiction.

The novel received generally favorable reviews. The *London Review of Books*, for instance, called it "a small masterpiece" that is "masterly by virtue of the credibility of her reconstruction of the contradictory emotions" and remarkable for a tone, which is "dry, like a newspaper reports of a crime, and at the same time crackling with life." The *Listener* praised it as "Bainbridgean domestic melodrama of the deepest dye and artistry" and "a wonderfully sad entertainment based on a popular form of Victorian crime." Similarly the reviewer in the *New York Times Book Review* saw it as an "enthralling novel about a pernicious marriage" and "a character study of terrible sad beauty." The review identified the novel as an "extraordinarily lively work of the imagination because the facts themselves remain so obdurately dull" but noted that Bainbridge was "a bit miserly with her sympathy for [Watson's wife,] Anne."[17]

Divided into five parts, *Watson's Apology* begins with a prologue—composed of six letters of introduction sent by John Selby Watson to Anne Armstrong in 1844 and a brief narrator's comment that these letters were exhibited as evidence in a trial thirty years later—and concludes with official documents describing the illness and death of Watson in 1884. Part 1, tracing events from 1844 to 1845, presents an account of the miserable days and impoverished conditions of Olivia and Anne Armstrong in Dublin. Reminiscent of the dreary and oppressive settings of *The Dressmaker* and *The Bottle Factory Outing*, Dublin's hardness and stasis, for the Armstrong sisters at least, encourage their antagonistic relationship with each other and a fatalistic, despairing view of their lives:

> A balcony, fronted with ornamental railings, ran the length of the double windows, but it was condemned as unsafe. Olivia had dryly remarked that this was a blessing, for had it been otherwise, Anne, in one of her moods, might have struggled out on to it and hurled herself into the street below. Escape, for either of them, was out of the question. Even in sleep they were flung together; their mattress sagged in the middle and the slightest shift in balance sent them rolling downhill like logs to the river. Existing as they did in such dreary proximity, Anne thought it hardly surprising that they were perpetually at war. (18)

Olivia, sickly, depressive, and possessing a "notoriously weak constitution" (19), is perceived as a detested but unavoidable burden by angry Anne, whose frequently clenched fists hint at her capacity for violence. Marriage, then, becomes an emblem of salvation for Anne. Whereas for John it signifies adherence to respectability and convention, for Anne it has merit as an avenue of escape. Accordingly Anne invents a reputable past and present in her reply letters to encourage her suitor's sympathy, while John strives to impress her with his sensitive poet's soul. If Bainbridge portrays Anne from unsympathetic angles, she depicts Watson as a complex mixture of aspirations and limitations: he is a poet with no lyricism, pedantic, an intellectual without intuition, a self-made figure eager to conform. The initial meeting of the pair, then, is not auspicious. Anne judges her future husband to be "a shade pompous, a shade dandified," and a man who looks "more like a prizefighter than a schoolmaster" (31); she also discerns that "he was arrogant and ambitious" (33). Watson sees merely "an insignificant little woman" (31). Although the scant attraction foreshadows the eventual antipathy of their marriage, Anne and John are nonetheless united by their needs; Watson's desire to expose "all the tribulations and longings he had known" (33) is matched by her need for release from Dublin and Olivia and by the erotic promise of marriage. Misgivings firmly denied, their marriage of mutual necessity proceeds hopefully. Although the fatalistic and pessimistic view of romance and marriage appears typical, Bainbridge's attention to mid-Victorian social and economic norms establishes the basis for the failure not only in human folly but also in inescapable external forces that limit freedoms and opportunities.

Part 2 begins eight years later and comprises four seasons, from summer 1853 to winter 1866. The rooms of the Watson house have become staked territories and the marriage a battleground. Despite the envisioned marital bounty, the quotidian reality is unappealing, marked by recriminations, guilt, anger, misunderstanding, jealousy, and suspicion. Watson, "a Gold Medallist in Classics and built like a bull" (57), dedicates himself to school duties and spends extracurricular hours writing translations of classical poetry—all of it the subject of "brutal reception" by critics (87). His cynicism about his seeming fate—he states, "To submit cheerfully to an existence that is unpleasing is only possible if one feels it to be temporary" (63)—results in further withdrawal from his wife and into his study. In contrast his bitter and often furious "neglected wife" (66) is unable to dispel her regrets and resentments or to give up her aspirations to partake in polite society. She concludes, "I have not come very far. . . . I have moved from one room with Olivia to two rooms with J. S. Watson" (75). Denied even "paltry treats" (73) such as occasional dinner parties or trips to the country, her resulting alienation and sadness, combined with the "ruthlessness of [her] Irish humour" (73), accelerates the marital quarreling.

The clashing of Anne's sensuality and inebriation with John's rationality and abstemiousness echoes the Dionysian/Apollonian struggle between the sisters of *The Dressmaker*. And as both static and oppositional forces, they seem likewise fated to eternal battle. As explicated by Bainbridge, moreover, the binding contract of marriage is a prison that also nurtures the worst traits of each half of the union. Marital domesticity becomes a long sequence of miserable scenes. For example, on the night Watson receives a commendation for twenty-two years of service as headmaster, he returns home to find her befuddled: "She was in her petticoats and there was a mauve stain on the front of her bodice. She was sixty years old and looked at him as though she believed she was a girl" (107). Following her declaration of love, he replies with aversion: "Sickened, he longed to tell her that love was not the problem. Love dropped out of the sky, unsought, unearned. He had loved his mother. It was liking somebody that was the difficulty" (108). The section concludes ominously with letters of employment termination and Watson's resignation.

In part 3 Bainbridge examines the increasing enmity within the marriage and the union's instability, heightened by reduced economic circumstances. The modest living affects each adversely; Anne's increasing untruthfulness, fury, and erratic behavior (ranging from accusations and tears to urinating in bed and hammering on the door of her husband's study) elicit little response from Watson, though he does confide to his friends that he had done Anne "great wrong" (120) by not ably providing for her. Bainbridge directs greater sympathy toward Watson, whose introspection leads to insight, though not action:

> He was miserably aware that his meanness of spirit was not due to the crushing disappointment he had suffered over the loss of his school, not to his lack of literary success, but rather to an accumulation of little wrongs done to him— a spoiled page, an intercepted letter, a burnt book. My marriage has destroyed me, he thought. I am buried under trivialities. (121)

With his last words to her, "You've not caused me to smile in twenty years" (132), he at last commits to criminal action. Subsequent to the discovery of Anne's corpse, Watson's friends and colleagues, like the novel's readers, strive to make sense of his behavior and question his sanity.

In the concluding two parts of *Watson's Apology*, set between 1872 and 1884, Bainbridge incorporates transcripts (including lengthy testimony by colleagues, neighbors, servants) from Watson's three-day trial, letters to the editor, and *Times* editorials. Bainbridge also envisions Watson's time in Parkhurst Prison on the Isle of Wight between 1872 and 1884 as invaluably introspective. There he takes time to recall his past and revise it. The novel closes with an unusual, fantastic recollection, the scene of the murder viewed by Watson as though a drama in which he did not participate. In that visionary moment, Watson observes a seemingly unrecognized man and woman quarreling and physically fighting. The man accuses the woman of being drunk, and she tells him, "You had nothing to give. . . . You're a cold fish" (221). The scene ends with a homicide and a transcendent experience:

> He took the gun from her and hit her repeatedly on the head. She clung to him, slithering down his chest, his stomach. A strand of her hair caught on his waistcoat buttons. She was moaning. He was horrified at the sound, and he hit her again and again to finish her off. . . .
>
> It was done now and he was glad. He had not harmed her, merely rid her of the bad things that had kept them apart.
>
> There was nothing in his head but light. He wondered if he was in the presence of God. He had never known anything so dazzling, so infinitely bright. (222)

In rendering the scene ambiguous—was killing Anne actually cathartic for Watson? Is his recollection and poetic reframing of it years later a technique of imparting meaning to a fundamentally spontaneous action? Is his excising of himself from his vision of the murder an indication of mental illness?—Bainbridge limits the clarity of her explanation of the crucial historical event of the novel. Although the author's note to *Watson's Apology* expresses a desire to supply character motives and feelings, this final moment suggests both the immense complexity of human character and action and the irreducibility of an act to one ultimate causality.

Comedy, Nostalgia, Pessimism: *An Awfully Big Adventure*

With *An Awfully Big Adventure* (1989), Bainbridge returned to the novel form, having published *English Journey* and her juvenile novella *Filthy Lucre* in the interim.[18] The novel's depressed Liverpool setting—a locale of decaying infrastructure and postwar deprivation that is populated by weary citizens with fresh memories of carnage and loss who are "used to such stories" (36)—recalls the similarly oppressive environments of *Young Adolf* and *The Dressmaker*. And its thematic features relating to self-deception, family, illusions, limitations, child rearing, and the past, echoed in the novel's frequent references to *Peter Pan*, are in keeping with Bainbridge's overarching examination of English society. Moreover the atmosphere of worn edges, alienation, fatigue, and looming violence stands in sharp contrast—in the manner of *Harriet Said* and *The Bottle Factory Outing*—to the bucolic expectation of the genre. Although the coming of age of Stella Bradshaw and her initiation into both adult relationships and the world of theater during the 1950s may imply promise of lighthearted nostalgia tinged with a literary playfulness introduced by the theater context, Bainbridge does not follow that conventional route; her depiction, emphatic in highlighting discord, miscommunication, deception, and social immobility, subverts genre norms.

In addition, with its forlorn air and disagreeable, unchanging characters, Bainbridge's novel conveys a darkly comic perspective, which numerous reviews observed. The *Times Literary Supplement* review called it a "cautionary tale" in which Bainbridge "employs her matter-of-fact Gothic technique" to render a "grim setting and characteristically bleak view of human nature." The *Listener* similarly judged it to be "a marvelous book, showing a novelist in absolute command of her material.

Fizzing with energy and black humour, it may be prescribed as the perfect post-Christmas pick-me-up." The reviewer for the *London Review of Books* considered the novel a "very believable portrait of the theatrical life," replete with "moving, funny and disturbing passages." Anita Brookner in the *Spectator* noted that Liverpool, "ugly, dirty, damaged and deprived," could be considered the novel's main character. Overall she admired the novel for its vision of "good quirky stuff" that is "recognizably if bizarrely English" and for its unique temperament, "the stuff of sadness, but sadness dressed up as grotesquerie." The reviewer then stated that *An Awfully Big Adventure* is "very strange novel indeed, gritty, sad, not quite realized" and that Bainbridge needs to "restore integrity to a style which is beginning to look arbitrary and a little threadbare."[19]

As in *The Dressmaker*, "0," the prologue of *An Awfully Big Adventure*, introduces the aftermath of an event that will lead to anxiety and recriminations when it unfolds at the novel's conclusion. This prologue also establishes a topography whose exhausted air reflects and, in turn, affects the characters:

> At this hour the square was empty. The flower-sellers had long since gone home, leaving the orange boxes piled up beside the urinal. Between the jagged buildings the lights of ships jumped like sparks above the river.
>
> They stood in silence, looking down into the darkness as though waiting for a curtain to rise. There was a sudden seep of orange light as the door of Brown's Café opened and the slattern in the gumboots staggered out to sling washing-up slops into the gutter. (2)

The novel then opens with characteristic family dynamics: claustrophobic closeness in a marginal business—"not exactly a hotel, more of a boarding house" (24)—that is home to embittered characters hemmed in by poverty, family history, scarcity, and limited economic options and social immobility. Although love and well wishing may be the principal motivation of each family member, the gap between intent and action is sizable. Instead of support and understanding, the family members—Uncle Vernon, Lily, and their ward Stella—are repeatedly shown sniping at one another; they frequently appear incapable of clearly conveying sympathetic responses, concern, or even their own states of mind. Worry about being shamed, caught, or judged by prying neighbors animates their consciousness, and that highly developed sense of propriety results in further disputes about proper public behavior. Moreover generational difference creates conflict between Stella and her foster parents. Conscious of their own inferior social standing (for example, Lily states, "People like us don't go to plays . . . let alone act in them" [9]), Uncle Vernon and Lily nonetheless believe that because Stella is not one of them, she is eligible for social ascent. Stella's beliefs are less secure.

Using the conventions of a coming-of-age narrative, Bainbridge begins the novel with parental discussion and scrutiny of Stella—of her character, weaknesses, and proper destiny. Reminiscent of Rita in *The Dressmaker*, Stella is viewed ambivalently, as a young woman with the potential to become successful but also as an impetuous individual who needs to rein in her emotions and curb her erratic enthusiasms. Bainbridge explicitly aligns her with performance, play acting, and posturing (22); she has at once a childlike innocence and an adult's manipulativeness. Stella possesses a "ferocious, if morbid, imagination" (10) and has a histrionic and willful temperament that is "constantly playing to the gallery" (11). She assumes "inappropriate" emotions that reflect an "almost comic" "false sensibility" (13); the "couplets of melancholy and madness that inflamed her imagination" (12) point to an adolescent's mercurial temperament and an artist's forceful personality. The family presumes that Stella, like her absent and maligned mother, Renée, is well suited to the "lush imagination of the theatre" (78). Despite their tentative faith, Bainbridge depicts moody and spiteful sixteen-year-old Stella as a mixture of qualities: she has been encouraged to stride toward the limelight by her Uncle Vernon, and although she firmly believes she knows what is expected of her, readers are told she possesses intelligence but not application and that she experienced failure earlier in school. The home atmosphere, associated with salvaged materials, borrowed goods, and inferior quality possessions, contributes its weight to her circumstance.

Bainbridge's episodic novel traces several months of Stella's immersion into the world of theater and adult relations, an experience that does not begin auspiciously. The theater itself is gloomy and unwelcoming, a "mixture of distemper, rabbit glue and damp clothing" (18). The expected associations with theater—imagination, creativity, magic—are replaced by a theater whose poorly lit, dirty, broken-down, and murky architecture suggests limitation and fettered, compromised creativity. Moreover the theater's staff is disappointingly ordinary, carrying with them petty quarrels, complicated histories, secrets, and various ulterior motives. Principal among them are Geoffrey, a nineteen-year-old student whom Stella believes is clever but "pig-ignorant" (31); Bunny, the stage manager; and Meredith Potter, a "man of the world" whom Stella believes she—like the cinema actresses she admires—will attract. Stella's involvement in what Geoffrey calls a "precarious profession" (104) is curiously uninspiring and mundane, especially because Bainbridge's focus is not on the magic of art and artifice but on rivalries, jealousies, competitions, romances within the company, and the technical problems and requirements of the various productions. In this unruly mixture of squabbles and provincial stagecraft, Stella's sudden and improbable attachment to Meredith, a much older man who has an unerring talent for choosing "inappropriate objects of desire" (49) and lacks the "capacity to sustain either love or hate" (60), seems commonplace.

The novel traces Stella's interactions with her colleagues and the ongoing uneasy relations with Uncle Vernon and Lily. As Stella learns the ropes and illustrates her naïveté and ignorance in numerous ways, Meredith decides to attend to her "spiritual welfare" (83); infatuated Stella, meanwhile, endeavors to transform herself into whatever she imagines he desires, "alter[ing] her demeanour several times a day" (85). Her close engagement with the adult world also introduces her to adult sexuality. Cast (like Bainbridge herself) as Ptolemy for a production of *Caesar and Cleopatra* and the subject of a newspaper interview emphasizing "'the local girl makes good' angle," Stella is astonished when the miserable reporter thrusts her hand inside his unbuttoned trousers. She adopts Meredith's "philosophical approach" for her overall predicament (which also includes unwanted attention from fellow thespians Richard St. Ives and Desmond Fairchild) and is "left holding a jelly baby of shriveled skin, her fingers glued together, webbed by a sticky emission" (91) while striving to remain dignified. Bainbridge later describes Stella's initial experience of sexual intercourse with O'Hara with much the same distaste. Rather than avoiding the man's advances, Stella capitulates, thinking, "It had to happen sometime and now was as good a time as any. She wanted to get it over with"

(172). After the consummation—"O'Hara climbed on top and humped her beneath the rude unshaded bulb" (173)—both lovers feel disappointed. His "momentary spasm of pleasure" is quickly forgotten, and she runs off, "almost chok[ing] on the stench of damp grain blowing up the hill" (174), in order to call her mother, who responds "in the usual way" (175).

Bainbridge's focus on Stella's initiation draws attention to odd comic events and behavior (for instance, Stella faints because of a massive boil on her neck, and a large crucifix is found tucked in her sock; later, feeling excluded from the close community, she is excited to be wandering through a derelict part of town where she encounters a man who frightens her by yelling at her; and still later she attempts calls her mother and finds her theater colleague Dawn Allenby passed out in the phone booth, having attempted suicide with an overdose of aspirin) and to the overall pathos of the theater players. Similarly a conversation during a celebratory meal is marked by unpleasant topics—neurosis, concentration camps, rancid stuffing—and leads to Stella's observation about her newfound friends: "All of them were alone" (168). Recently highlighted in *Young Adolf* and *Winter Garden*, this vision of individuals as deformed recurs throughout Bainbridge's work, beginning with the cruel outlandishness of Claude, Norman, and Shebah in *A Weekend with Claude*. In such a perplexing and discouraging social setting, Stella's attempts to develop friendships and love unsurprisingly range from desultory to comically misguided.

The novel's episodic structure in fact depicts scene after scene of social interaction marred by miscommunication, selfishness, and unmet expectations. Uncle Vernon's gruesome war story ruining Christmas dinner is only one example of many. And the dysfunction of family is matched by the dysfunction of her newly formed adult attachments in the theater. Stella's second sexual engagement with O'Hara is remarkable for the misunderstandings, exasperation, and awkwardness it produces. And the more time they spent together, the greater the barriers grow between them. When O'Hara reveals that he is married, for example, Stella offhandedly mentions that she is in love with someone else. Despite abundant signs that the liaison is destined for failure, the pair continue to meet; Stella's indifference is complemented by O'Hara's bafflement: "He couldn't make her out, or himself for that matter. What had started as an unimportant if rather shameful seduction had become something altogether more painful. He had lost his heart and was in danger of losing his head" (186).

An Awfully Big Adventure concludes with a looming sense of disintegration and a transition from adolescence to adulthood that has uncertain significance. Bainbridge reveals secrets that reinforce the impression of the fragility or inherent corruption of relationships. During the visit of a famous comedian, which culminates in a mock football game and an altercation between Meredith and Geoffrey, Stella, bored, watches a funeral procession, imagines Uncle Vernon in the coffin, and concludes that death would not be "an awfully big adventure" (189) for him. The altercation between the men is soon revealed to be a lover's quarrel. At another chamber in the theater's "nest of intrigue" (192), O'Hara is reminded that it is a "criminal offence to consort with a minor" (193). O'Hara subsequently learns of Stella's illegitimacy and her illusory phone calls to her mother, Renée, an aspiring actor who, before her abrupt move to the United States, had won a part to be the "speaking clock out of the whole of England" (201).

Bainbridge's dark comic rendering emphasizes both partially revealed knowledge and dire repercussions. When O'Hara, for example, states, "Life is full of conflagrations. . . . We can never be sure when we'll be consumed by the past" (200), Lily thinks, "He had a lovely way of talking, but then, he was an actor" (201), and thereby calls into question the legitimacy of his insight. O'Hara realizes he had known Stella's mother. Minutes later he strikes his skull when he slips on an oil streak and, lying on the ground, attempts to "get rid of that image of the girl he had known as Stella Maris holding a baby in her arms" (202). His panicky response suggests that he is Stella's father. The final scene depicts the concluding moments of *Peter Pan* in which Tinkerbell is supposed to be revived by the children's belief in fairies: "For a moment the clapping continued, rose in volume, then died raggedly away, replaced by a tumult of weeping." The weeping, presumably coming from the cast in response to O'Hara's accident (or death) and the audience because Tinkerbell does not immediately revive, contrasts sharply with the comic affirmation of the play. The final segment of *An Awfully Big Adventure*, an untitled, single-page epilogue, echoes the scene in "0" in which Stella confides, "It wasn't my fault" to a stranger in order to obtain coins for the pay phone. She then listens to her mother, a recorded voice that says "the usual thing": The "pretty mother" informs her daughter that the time "is 6.47 and 20 seconds precisely" (205). As shaped by Bainbridge the coming-of-age narrative culminates only in befuddled adulthood. Although Stella has reached a maturity of sorts, her incomplete knowledge, instability, and discouraging environment are foreboding, promising little other than further confusion and discontent.

CHAPTER 6

Fictions of History

The Birthday Boys, Every Man for Himself,
Master Georgie, and *According to Queeney*

Q: But you'd want to think of your writing as having
   some sort of enduring significance, wouldn't you?
   You'd want to see it as containing some higher
   truths?

A: Higher truths? Oh no. Not at all. If it has any higher
   significance, it's only to me and not to anyone else.
   Had I not written my books I would probably have
   been in a mental home by now. Writing gets rid of
   everything. That is the only reason I ever began to
   write. I wanted to write out things that happened in
   childhood. There was no other reason at all. And
   now I'm going through a dilemma. I've done all that
   stuff about childhood. It's all written out. And then
   I thought I would do the history books. And that
   meant getting a different voice. And that was difficult. But now I've decided that I can't repeat myself
   with another history thing so I will set my next novel
   in the 1950s. And I found that the me that was there
   before has totally gone. I can't find me any more.

Q: You can't find the emotions?

A: No, I can't find the voice. For me that is the emotions. Whatever I am has completely disappeared. I
   keep thinking, where am I? I can't hear any voices

from the fifties. I'm wondering if those people,
including me, don't exist anymore.

Beryl Bainbridge, *New Humanist*,
5 January 2004

After *An Awfully Big Adventure,* Bainbridge has published
historical novels exclusively. Though the subjects she chooses—the
Scott expedition (1910–12), the days leading to the sinking of the
Titanic (8–15 April 1912), the Crimean War (1853–56), and the
final years of Samuel Johnson (1765–84)—have national significance, marked visibility, or notoriety in British history, her attention to them is neither jingoistic nor nationalistic and epic. Instead
she frequently pays less attention to the specific details and developments of the historical moment itself than to the domestic
details of the relationships between the hapless and frequently perplexed individuals caught up in it. The significance of the event
in a conventionally historiographic sense, then, is overlooked in
favor of an examination of individuals and their relationships in
context to it. For instance, much of *Every Man for Himself* takes
place days *before* the *Titanic* sinks on 15 April 1912. Similarly,
although the senseless carnage of England's war with Russia in the
Crimea is depicted in *Master Georgie*, Bainbridge's portrait of it
does not attend to the chronology of the historical event per se or
to what it meant to England and the balance of power. Instead it
observes complex relations within a small social group whose
involvement with war is often tangential.

Moreover Bainbridge's prismatic storytelling—three narrators in *Master Georgie*, multiple points of view in *According
to Queeney*, five discrete journal-like segments written by expedition members in *The Birthday Boys*—emphasizes subjectivity and knowledge gaps: already holding personal biases that
color their interpretations of what they do directly observe, her

characters also have incomplete understanding of the event in which they take part. Taken together, the limitations and lack of objectivity bring to mind Bainbridge's statement in *Forever England* about the concealing, omission, and distortion of historiography and the necessarily subjective nature of truth. Furthermore her skepticism about truth and her wariness about the politics of representation align her with a late-twentieth-century literary development whose British practitioners include John Fowles, A. S. Byatt, Julian Barnes, Jeanette Winterson, Margaret Drabble, and Peter Ackroyd. As explained by Frederick Holmes (who is summarizing influential accounts proposed by Brian McHale and Linda Hutcheon), this contemporary variant of the historical novel maintains an ambivalent relationship to its own aims:

> The paradox inheres in the way such works create a vivid illusion of the unfolding of historical events, involving people who actually existed, only to dispel the illusion by laying bare the artifice that give rise to it. In contrast, traditional historical novels sustain throughout the pretence of supplying direct access to the past in all its fullness and particularity. . . . As Brian McHale says, whereas traditional historical novels "typically involve some violation of ontological boundaries," they "strive to suppress these violations, to hide the ontological 'seams' between fictional projections and real world facts." It is, of course, just these "seams" which postmodern historical fiction is intent to flaunt.[1]

Holmes implies that postmodern historical novelists have explicitly political, nearly programmatic, and apparently didactic aims for their fiction. The same cannot be said as readily of Bainbridge's recent novels. Though her historical fiction can be seen as conventional because its realism appears to be "supplying direct access to the past in all its fullness and particularity," its subversive narrating strategies, like much postmodern historical fiction, flout those same conventions.

National Calamity I: *The Birthday Boys*

The Birthday Boys (1991), set between June 1910 and March 1912, is narrated in five discrete sections by members of the failed Scott expedition to the South Pole.[2] By focusing on the personality and perspective of each man—Petty Officer Edgar Evans, Dr. Edward Wilson, Captain Robert Falcon Scott, Lieutenant Henry Robertson Bowers, and Captain Lawrence Edward Oates—along a chronology that begins with the launch of their ship in Cardiff and concludes with the final hours of the expedition, Bainbridge traces the shift from exaltation to fear as the expedition's losses of equipment, provisions, and direction become calamitous, and she examines group tensions and differing points of view about the expedition's leadership. That variety of perspectives also enables Bainbridge to offer five differing accounts of both Scott's leadership and of the conditions and society experienced over five (of twenty-two) months. If the Scott expedition was "the worst journey in the world" (as it is called in Apsley Cherry-Garrard's renowned 1922 account of that name), then Bainbridge's treatment of it chooses to ponder the minutia, directing attention to its moments instead of evaluating its significance. In contrast to her earlier depictions of individuals and social interactions, moreover, Bainbridge's approach is notable for its sympathetic rendering and refusal of comic caricature.

Reviews in general applauded Bainbridge's effort. The *Spectator* commented on the charitable portrayal of Scott and called

The Birthday Boys a "beautiful piece of storytelling" that "most valuably . . . teaches compassion for fallen heroes." In the *New York Times Book Review,* Gary Krist called the novel "extra-ordinary" and suggested that one of its goals is to debunk "sentimentalized views of the figures from our past." He commended Bainbridge for her sensitivity: "Bringing her subversive and ever-mischievous imagination to bear to the subject, she fills in details neglected by Scott's diary, deepening the portrait of stiff-upper-lip heroism by adding the sometimes ugly shadows that suggests real life." Krist also viewed the novel as having broadly political goals, stating that it "does imply a critique of something more than just the so-called 'Heroic Age of Polar exploration.' It seems to pass judgment on the whole ethos of action, conquest and empire upon which so much of European history has been based." The *London Review of Books* noted that Bainbridge is truly concerned with myths, but because she does not wish to appear serious, she is regarded as a lightweight author. Admiring the novel overall, D. J. Enright nonetheless expressed a desire for the author to forego "seductive dottiness" and "try just a little harder" to make a grand literary gesture. The *Times Literary Supplement* review, referring to the numerous accounts of the Scott expedition published over the decades, observed, "Imagination has a difficult journey to go to reach [the Scott expedition members], one complicated by the busy work imagination has been doing on them for eighty years," and noted that although Bainbridge's "brush is broad and comic," the novel is "sensitive and acute" (though from "the ventriloquistic point of view, she isn't entirely successful").[3]

The two opening sections of *The Birthday Boys,* narrated by Evans and Wilson, establish the stratified relations among the ship's crew as well as introduce incidental material about the expedition itself. In describing their personal experiences, the narrators of these sections also illustrate the national and imperial significance of the expedition. Evans, in charge of scientific and polar journey equipment and a bawdy storyteller with a penchant for exaggeration and embroidery despite his claims to utter "the gospel truth" (9), expresses an awareness of his inferior class position and the disparity it engenders (for example, he notes that he is "careful to smile with the right amount of deference" [12] when speaking with Scott). As an acute observer of human character, he also serves to introduce the leadership of the expedition, with its rivalries and interpersonal politics. Observing Scott and Wilson, for instance, he notes how "both of them come from what the privileged classes assume to be humble backgrounds, meaning that from guilt, temperament or ill winds blown up by life's vicissitudes they've felt compelled to earn a living" (12–13), and that he has "come to the conclusion the Doctor pursues his chosen course on account of spiritual leanings, whereas the Owner's driven by necessity" (13). He judges Dr. Wilson to be a peacemaker tempering Scott, who becomes angry and "nervy" because "he's burdened with such heavy responsibilities" (13). Furthermore, although Evans concludes that Scott is a "forever gentleman" (36), he is critical enough of him to discern that he is "overburdened with emotions" (14). He expresses skeptical regard for Scott's term "great enterprise" but accepts that he is "part of something special, something with glory in it" (41). Elsewhere, Evans proclaims the faults of the ship, laments the differences between men and women and how their "minds remain wretchedly unaligned" (29), and ponders the "heady feel of being famous," which is mitigated by the question of "whether we'll be on that final march to plant the flag" (34). His wary sensibility, delineated by

Bainbridge of course, is aptly Bainbridgean: "It's the old business of the rotten apple in the barrel. We all lean toward contagion" (35).

Taking place one month after Evans's, Dr. Wilson's narration, that of a dispassionate gentleman, takes note of scenery, examines and catalogs species, and offers up anthropological speculation. He comments about the invigorating value of labor and the "congenial" (51) nature of his travel companions. Solitary, pedantic, and scholarly, a man who had considered becoming a missionary and is considered "something of a dull fish" (54), his rational discourse is interspersed with theology and assorted scientific speculations. The commentary—that their "ancient ship leaks like a sieve" (53), about weather conditions and grouse disease—illuminates both Wilson's and Evans's dissimilarity and the educated man's notions of gentlemanly pursuits. The doctor also recalls past expeditions and confides that the expedition members "are the misfits, victims of a changing world" in which ideas they were taught to value, such as "love of country, of Empire, of devotion to duty," are "being held up to ridicule" (64). For Wilson the movement away from the ancient standards of English society seems regrettable: "The validity of the class system, the motives of respectable, educated men are now as much under scrutiny of the magnifying glass as the parasites feeding off the Scottish grouse" (64). Wilson's recollections of past expeditions also reveal the importance of such expeditions to (imperialist) English society. The wry portraiture here is as close as Bainbridge stands to comic mockery in the novel.

Bainbridge places Captain Scott's narration as the pivotal middle chapter of the novel. Scott's section, dated March 1911, offers an account of the expedition as it approaches land and its goal. Its literal centrality is significant too, insofar as it reflects

Scott's own rank as the planner and leader of the expedition and the figure—a symbol, a national hero—associated with its eventual failure. Moreover the opening sentences—"Having to sail on past Cape Crozier came as a frightful blow. I'd banked on establishing our winter quarters there, but it proved impossible to land owing to the swell" (81)—emphasize unexpected difficulties and flawed calculations ("All my plans and calculations had been made" [81]; "I must admit it was something I hadn't taken into account" [83]; "It's obvious a serious mistake was made in the selection" [89]) that foreshadow the disastrous conclusion of the expedition and the occasionally irresolute temperament of its leader.

As with the previous narratives, Bainbridge depicts individuals pondering a mixed assortment of topics, observations, and ideas. Scott's meandering focus—which includes the team's being plagued by "infernal bad luck" (88) and "damnable bad luck" (103), the massive storms, the setbacks (such as snow blindness of his men, pack-animal limitations, and machinery failure), the monotony of the experience ("Each day begins very much like the last" [91], Scott complains), and his stomach difficulties, which according to his wife are the result of "undigested conflicts" (93)—clarifies the arduousness, difficulty, danger, and exhilaration of the journey. Furthermore Scott reveals his sense of being in competition with his former junior office, Shackleton, and he judges his Norwegian rival, Amundsen, to be "absolutely appalling" in character: "His duplicity, his lack of sportsmanship leaves me shuddering with disgust" (102). Scott becomes incensed because Amundsen "just wants to make a race of it" instead of being "interested in science" (102). Like the previous narrators, Scott, who is speculative, rigorous, rational, self-consciously civilized, and decorous, dedicates time to thinking about his place in society and about modernity and what it signifies. He upholds the value of civility and Englishness, for example, when he encounters litter: "All the same, I cannot understand the mentality of people so shallow, so lacking in foresight as to act in such a manner. Surely it's a mark of civilized human behaviour to leave a place in the condition one would wish to find it" (82). Likewise, when he declares, "Bravery is a conscious act of discipline. . . . And as far as I'm concerned there are worse things than dying. Cowardice for one" (97), he aligns himself with familiar Victorian ideals of (English) gentlemanly deportment.

Even so, as the expedition plods forward, Scott expresses frequent self-doubt and uncertainty about the feasibility of their goal: "The whole expedition is terribly unwieldy for one man to run. Perhaps we were too ambitious . . . perhaps I should have brought more dogs and less ponies" (103). Conditions and morale worsen, and he confesses that he is not himself (104); he returns to sanity under Wilson's tutelage. When he gives a speech to the crew, saying, "We must go on, without fear or panic, and do our best for the honour of our country," he also states, "I sounded convincing" (104). His maintaining of appearances disguises deep-rooted malaise: "I didn't let on, but I fancied there was something broken in me, some spring that no longer worked" (105). In Scott's worried view, the expedition fast becomes "a losing battle" with sick animals, destructive weather, and low morale. His insistent justifications ("I'd underestimated the effects. . . . It's surely unprecedented, and I don't see how I could have taken it into account" [109]; "Nobody will ever convince me that the stars don't play a part in it" [111]) add to the discordant atmosphere in which the men—"more than a little overwrought" (114) and not in their "right minds" (114)—seek leadership from a figure trapped by unyielding circumstances. In mental isolation Scott strives to make "plans for the Polar journey" (115) and ponders how to contend with the expedition's "weak links" (118). His narrative concludes during Taff's birthday celebration with uncertainty and unsettling thoughts of his wife.

The final two segments of *The Birthday Boys*, narrated by Lieutenant Henry Robertson Bowers (dated July 1911) and Captain Lawrence Edward Oates (dated March 1912), respectively, offer accounts of the further "bad luck" and inhospitable conditions the expedition encounters. From section to section, Bainbridge's focus on differing perspectives and perceptions within the group subtly draws attention to any reader's ultimate ability to fully know "the truth" about the event being narrated. Bowers's narration, a chronicle of a side trip to a penguin rookery at Cape Crozier, adds another stratum to an already stratified tale. Bowers recounts the initial excitement—"We thought this an awfully big adventure" (135)—which is soon tempered by sober assessment: "As early as the first day I think both Bill and I began to realize what we'd let ourselves in for" (135). Less introspective and speculative than Scott and Wilson, Bowers maintains his attention on the details of each day, such as the hardships caused by weather and illness. Frequently lyrical— "We took hours to make camp and hours to break camp, and in between tottered like children across the immensity of that bleak and hiemal playground" (137); "We were like flies fluttering against a window that would never open" (148)—the narration nonetheless establishes the oppressive, life-threatening environment that envelops them.

Encountering blizzards and temperatures in the minus sixties over the nineteen-day trek to Cape Crozier (about which, Bowers notes, "That first, awful week we thought conditions had got about as bad as we could encounter, and we were wrong" [140]), the men, and Bowers in particular, maintain a hopeful and enthusiastic demeanor. Despite the adversities, for instance, Bowers emphasizes the rightness of the "jolly worthy enterprise" (139) of collecting penguin eggs. Although acknowledging the possibility that he may be clinging to outmoded and "inappropriate chivalry of a bygone age," Bowers maintains a belief that there is "something splendid, sublime even, in pitting oneself against the odds" (144). Seeing himself as a man born on the cusp of change toward societal mechanization and "into the last few seconds of an epoch in which a man is still required to stand up and be counted," he is also relieved by a reprieve in the weather and attributes it to God: "I understood then that providence was on our side; it was unthinkable to believe that God would save us simply to prolong the agony" (145). A few days later he reiterates his belief that "God has something in store for us, something glorious" (157). Sometimes crazed and delirious, Bowers does live to narrate his return to the main camp. Though his birthday remains unacknowledged, Bowers concludes his narrative with a testimony to the fraternity between the men. To Wilson's statement, "I could not have found two better companions, and what is more, I never shall," Bowers replies, "It may be that the purpose of the worst journey in the world had been to collect eggs which might prove a scientific theory, but we'd unraveled a far greater mystery on the way—the missing link between God and man is brotherly love" (158). The journey ends with their return to Cape Evans and the discovery of three men encased in ice.

Describing scenes about eight months later, Captain Oates's narration, that of a man whose "world is no longer large enough to contain anyone but [him]self" (161), dwells on the loss of equipment and animals as well as other members of the expedition. Bainbridge envisions how deprivation and desperation have their effects on morale. Oates especially is full of recriminations about Scott's "catalogue of disasters and miscalculations" (163). To Scott's refrain of "bad luck," he counters, "I've never known such a man for making mistakes and shifting the blame onto others" (163). But even with his critical regard for Scott, Oates is eager to partake in the final leg of their quest to the pole, describing the excitement and optimism before quickly turning his attention to the "dither" (178) that entangles Scott soon after and the "dreadful circumstances" (178–79) that their leader refuses to address. Upon discovering that Amundsen had reached the pole before them, the group turns back, their sense of accomplishment undermined. The final few segments of Oates's increasingly disjointed narration reflect his sense of lost time and record the steady increase of mishaps and diminishing ability to cope with their environment. He points out Scott's "fatal course" in choosing to move eastward (182) but admits that Scott is the only one capable of decisions, as Wilson, Birdie, and Evans have been handicapped by weather and injury. At the beginning stage of gangrene, Oates understands that he will soon die. On the day before what he guesses is his birthday, he asks Dr. Wilson for morphine because he does not want to "end screaming" (187). Scott orders Wilson to give him the tablets; after a night of vivid dreams he wakes up and decides to go outside. Delirious, he hears a man singing, "Happy Birthday" and exclaims, "And oh, how warm it was" (189).

Juxtaposed to the disastrous yet unexpectedly mirthful conclusions of *Injury Time*, *Winter Garden*, and *The Bottle Factory Outing*, the final scenes of *The Birthday Boys* are remarkable for their grim realism and their sympathetic and accepting characterization. In place of the deeply flawed and disagreeable characters of her social novels, Bainbridge presents figures that, although no moral paragons, embody admirable qualities and commendable beliefs. Furthermore, as a fictional account of a historical event, *The Birthday Boys* veers away from offering an explanation of the expedition's failings that may have escaped historical inquiry and from identifying the expedition's significance to British history. Characteristically, Bainbridge's vignettes of the expedition focus on interpersonal relationships and the relationship between individuals and the frequently inhospitable cosmos. If, in novels such as *Injury Time* and *Winter Garden*, the cruelty of that cosmos seemed an apt punishment for ethically compromised and foolish characters, the relationship is not the same in *The Birthday Boys*. Instead Bainbridge conveys empathy and admiration for both the ambitions of the men and their varied responses to certain death.

National Calamity II: *Every Man for Himself*

Captain Oates's narration concludes during March 1912, and Bainbridge's subsequent novel, *Every Man for Himself* (1996), winner of the Whitbread Award for Best Novel, opens on 15 April 1912.[4] Over five sections, dated 8 April to 15 April 1912, the novel represents one man's account of the days preceding the sinking of the renowned if ill-fated luxury liner. Opening with a description of the narrator's experience with an unnamed man moments before the stranger leapt from the deck into the water, the novel's point of view, as with *The Birthday Boys*, enables Bainbridge to focus less on the historical, national, or symbolic significance of the event than on portraying the minutia of the social networks and individual experiences aboard the ship. The author's characteristic interest, then, remains directed at scrutinizing complicated and seldom placid relationships. Moreover, like *Young Adolf, Winter Garden*, and *Injury Time, Every Man for Himself* depicts strange happenings, inexplicable behaviors, and bizarre characters—all of which either confound the narrator or convince him of the surreal instability of his world. A derisive or despairing comic perspective commonly accompanies Bainbridge's surreality, but in *Every Man for Himself* the comic has a scant but detectable presence that is subordinate to a cross-class depiction of ordinary albeit complex social engagements aboard the doomed vessel.

Examined as a critique of "early twentieth century notions of class and gender," the novel was met with some ambivalence by reviewers.[5] For instance, the *London Review of Books* reviewer, calling the author "a cross between a witch and a clown," was confounded by the numerous mysteries of the plot and concluded that Bainbridge "seems to have decided to disturb her readers without moving them." The reviewer noted too many "two-dimensional characters" and likened the novel to "an upmarket disaster movie." Likewise, the *Times Literary Supplement* review expressed concern that Bainbridge's intentions were "too much in shadow" and "we never really care about the destiny of any" of the characters, that "her wonderfully idiosyncratic roughness and singularity of point of view are less in evidence here than we should like," and that "the book's deep layers are too easily allowed to go down with the ship." John Updike in the *New Yorker* pointed out the "somewhat bizarre and ghostly swarm of characters" and complained that "Bainbridge writes with a kind of betranced confidence, seeming to lose all track of her story only to pop awake for a stunning image or an intense exchange." The *Spectator* lauded that novel's conclusion as "superb" even though the story was "over-loaded somewhat by [the protagonist's] melodramatic personal history." In the *New York Times Book Review* Janet Kaye stated that it is "difficult to imagine a more engrossing account of the famous shipwreck than this one" and praised the novel's illustra-tion of "death rites not only for a ship but for an entire way of life."[6]

Bainbridge begins the novel by highlighting her narrator, Morgan, and his unusual circumstances. Aboard the *Titanic* he recalls a strange event that occurred a few days previously: "At half-past four on the afternoon of 8th April 1912—the weather was mild and the hyacinths bloomed in window boxes—a stranger chose to die in my arms" (11). The death prompts a further recollection that when he was ten he "met a man who blew his head off" (15). Morgan alludes to other "grotesque happenings" (14) in his childhood that led him to believe that he was "special" and "destined to be a participant rather than a spectator of singular events" (15). Bainbridge establishes Mor-gan as a young man in a precarious social position, both inside and outside of polite society. An orphan, he was raised by a wealthy and high-status family, yet he has no assurance about his continued acceptance within well-heeled society. In addition he suffers from a generational ennui. An apprentice draftsman who had worked on a small aspect of the design of the *Titanic*, Mor-gan takes little interest in the massive liner. He is restless for stimulation and seemingly feckless; he appears to be an embod-iment of spoiled and thankless youth. In fact, as Morgan settles into C deck and speaks to his Scottish steward, McKinlay, he proclaims himself "young and in need of sensation" (27) at age twenty-two. The posture, reminiscent of the Bright Young Things of Waugh or Hemingway, is cynical and weary: "We had spent our lives in splendid houses and grand hotels and for us there was nothing new under the sun" (36). In spite of his seeming apathy Morgan reveals himself to be open to enthusiasms. The "sublime thermodynamics" of the *Titanic*, for example, affect him deeply: "Dazzled, I was thinking that if the fate of man was connected to the order of the universe, and if one could equate the scientific workings of the engines with such a reciprocal universe, why then, nothing could go wrong with my world" (36). His ambivalence is evident when he reports his friend Melchett's admiration of the magnificent wonders of the ship—"A cathedral . . . constructed of steel and capable of carrying a congregation of three thousand souls across the Atlantic" (31)—and he feels that he has momentarily "loosened that grey veil of sophistication common to our kind" (33). That ennui indicates his class-borne need for stimulation, his sense of purposelessness, and his belief that he ought to have a greater destiny than he currently possesses. As a variant of a coming of age narrative, moreover, *Every Man for Himself* portrays Morgan undergoing mettle-testing trials whose outcomes reveal the sort of adult he will become.

Over the days preceding the *Titanic*'s collision, Bainbridge maintains focus on Morgan's complicated social interactions and personal crises. Chief among the interactions is his growing relationship with disfigured and enigmatic Scurra, who falsely claims that his scarred mouth is a result of "discourse with a macaw" (38) when he was young. Though Morgan initially imagines that Scurra will be "someone [he] might usefully cultivate" (18), he soon realizes that the man's robust appearance is distinct from his murky interior. Nonetheless Scurra offers an inviting warmth of manner to Morgan, whose male friends "kept each other at a distance" (76). Morgan, mortified when

Scurra asks, "What does it matter what anyone thinks?" (79), also learns of the relativity of manners and ideologies via Scurra, who often takes an antagonistic or skeptical stance when he hears Morgan's uncritical acceptance of the status quo. Untethered if not fully disconnected from his social stratum, Morgan's gimlet-eyed regard for the "smart set" (43) reveals the obfuscating role of manners and etiquette; behind the facade he takes note of scandals and excess drinking, family upsets, and stupidity. In fact, in his discontent Morgan comes to see his privileged world as one "big unhappy family" (73): "The world consists of men who know us. Look around you. This place is chock-a-block with people who went to the same schools, the same universities, attended the same fencing classes, shared the same dancing masters, music teachers, Latin tutors, tennis coaches" (72).

In part 3, dated "Friday 12th April," Morgan's leisurely day includes domestic activities, social outings, and a "warning of ice ahead" (102) during a tour of the "marvels of modern technology" (104) the ship bears. Although Bainbridge does allude to the impending disaster, her focus on the historical moment remains fixed on the ephemeral and quotidian. After all, from Morgan's perspective (and that of the others on the *Titanic*) the days are extraordinary only insofar as they are aboard a magnificent ship. Bainbridge's novel, then, continues to trace Morgan's meandering itinerary: he lunches with Scurra, who dismisses Morgan's beliefs in democracy and "a new way of living" (107), calling him "rich, pompous, [and] ignorant of the lives of the general mass of humanity" (108); he has a quarrel with a male acquaintance and another with the object of his infatuation, Wallis; and he decides on letter writing and reading Shakespeare but quickly abandons his determined path. Scurra later reveals that he saw Morgan's mother serving tables in a restaurant in Provence years ago. The revelations about his mother's alcoholism and his adoption by the subsequently poisoned Miss Barrow provoke Morgan. Still later in the evening he enters further discussion with the mysterious Scurra about women, love, betterment of the working class, and the proper uses of wealth. He concludes the day by noting that six ice warnings having been logged over the past twenty-four hours.

Bainbridge maintains consistent focus on the volatile ephemera of each day, effectively encouraging an understanding of the *Titanic* disaster that strips it of its emblematic or symbolic status. Moreover her rendering of Morgan's daily interactions is consistent with the critical vision of humanity presented across numerous novels, beginning with *A Weekend with Claude*. Whether depicting 1971, 1874, or 1912, Bainbridge foregrounds humanity as flawed, conflicted, fractious, and prone to misunderstandings and misguided actions. Accordingly Morgan's next day is a typical mixture of provocative communication, misunderstandings, anxiety, and unresolved complications. Waking "distinctly uneasy" on 13 April, Morgan begins his day with an intense breakfast conversation with Rosenfelder, who accuses his friends of abnormality brought on by wealth—though Rosenfelder claims that Morgan is different because he has a conscience (143). Fretful with anxiety about Wallis, Morgan begins drinking; he later hears Wallis and Scurra exchanging coarse sexual words in her stateroom. Filled with humiliation and rage, Morgan expresses his relief at being able to escape the scene without detection. A subsequent confrontation with Scurra reveals Morgan's outraged sense of honor and decorum being met directly with Scurra's indifference: "'My dear boy,' [Scurra] said. 'Have you not yet learnt that it's every man for himself?'"

(154). The next morning he awakes with the realization that "nothing lasts, neither joy nor despair," and feels refreshed having "banished the whole shameful business" (157) from his mind. Introspective Morgan, determining himself to be a newly "serious man" (159) committed to adult concerns, has his attention redirected when his room shakes as the ship hits an iceberg. Despite the passengers' initial excitement, crew calculations reveal that the ship will sink in less than two hours.

The final section of *Every Man for Himself*, dated "Monday, 15th April," begins with Morgan's speculation about individual response to calamity and adverse conditions: "There is no way of knowing how one will react to danger until one is faced with it. Nor can we know what capacity we have for nobility and self-sacrifice unless something happens to rouse such conceits into activity" (181). Asked to help with the loading of the lifeboats and to keep the truth of the ship's rate of sinking from fellow passengers, Morgan comprehends that too few lifeboats, too little preparation, bad communication resulting from the ship's size, and incredulousness founded on the firm, widely held belief that "the ship is unsinkable" (185) will lead to chaos and casualties. His involvement with Wallis, Scurra, and others during the "terrible confusion" (200) reveals a nascent sense of compassion and selflessness.

The section concludes with scenes of the ship listing and the crowd growing unruly and fearful. The boat sinks: "Then silence fell, and that was the worst sound of all. There was no trace of the *Titanic*. All that remained was the grey veil of vapour drifting above the water" (222). In a collapsible lifeboat floating wrong side up, Morgan sits with "twenty or more, lying like sponges in the icy pond within that canvas bag, looking up at the stars, students of the universe, each lost in separate thoughts and dreams" (222). Waiting within the pale fleet of ice islands, they greet morning—and with it the arrival of the smoking stack of a rescue ship. Bainbridge's final image is ambiguous, suggestive of hope and loss. Morgan's unusual and discomfiting experiences over the preceding day, moreover, remain unprocessed by the narration. What they signify and how they will affect him in the future are uncertain. As with *The Birthday Boys*, Bainbridge's historical novel is marked by an insistent focus on unexceptional (if characteristically Bainbridgean) social interaction and diverse responses to hostile conditions. Uninterested in didacticism—in drawing a history lesson, for instance, or assessing the historical significance of a discrete event—Bainbridge's evocation of a few days aboard the *Titanic* instead observes the behavior of a small group of historically remote characters whose clashes of perspective and ideology, crises of miscommunication, and intermittent moments of communion just happen to occur aboard the age's most magnificent and ill-fated vessel.

National Calamity III: *Master Georgie*

Master Georgie (1998), set in England and Crimea between 1846 and 1854, observes war from oblique angles and takes the titular figure, a wealthy surgeon and amateur photographer, as its principal focus.[7] Over six chapters (each named after a photographic tableau created by the principal characters), Bainbridge portrays scenes from the life and death of George Hardy. As with the numerous narrators of *The Birthday Boys*, the points of view of Bainbridge's three narrators, Myrtle, Pompey Jones, and Dr. Potter (notable as well for being split along lines of class and gender), enable readers to study differing perspectives about a figure, a society, and an international event. Recalling Bainbridge's comment about all truth being subjective, the novel's narration and its fabulous photographic representations also prompt recollection of Hutcheon's postmodern historical fiction and its "problematizing of the nature of historical knowledge."[8] Interpreted as a "carefully planned attack on the concept of a heroic war narrative," the novel's storytelling also subtly undermines its own seamlessness as quasi-historiographic representation.[9]

Again the reviews were full of praise. The *London Review of Books* viewed the novel as portraying "a world of instability and mortality" and concluded that "nothing about this novel is simple or easy, though its brevity, and the fact that it's so readable sometimes makes it seem both." The reviewer for the *New York Times Book Review* compared Bainbridge's novels to "elegant teacups that contain a strong, dark, possibly sinister but remarkable brew" and focused on the novel's "companionable alliance between wry, deadpan humor and nightmarish horror" before concluding that the novel is "hardly a feel-good book—unless you're a reader whose spirits are lifted by the prospect of a writer so original and so firmly in control of her art." Calling the novel a "triumph" featuring "pleasingly grotesque scenes," the *Spectator* reviewer claimed that to "find fault isn't easy" but pointed out a few anachronisms. In the *Times Literary Supplement* reviewer David Horspool stated that considering the novel's subject was "so difficult to comprehend," Bainbridge ought to be commended for rendering it "immediate and vivid, and as chaotic, as anything set in the present."[10]

The first chapter, "Plate 1. 1846 Girl in the Presence of Death," is narrated by the eventual "Girl" captured for posterity in George's photographic plate dated 1846. Myrtle, a foundling who cannot "recollect a mother and never had a birthday until the Hardy family took [her] in" (9), was named after the street where her would-be orphanage home stood in Liverpool; fate, in the form of a smallpox epidemic, intervened and directed her instead to the home of Mr. Hardy. She had been discovered in a cellar "beside the body of a woman whose throat had been nibbled by rats" (9). Liverpool—the squalid, decaying, and harsh city evident in *An Awfully Big Adventure, Young Adolf,* and *The Dressmaker*—has produced in Myrtle an adaptable, matter-of-fact, eager, and dedicated figure. Despite these seemingly dispassionate and rational qualities, Myrtle's enduring love for George gives her life its direction. As the novel opens Myrtle is recalling the first time she was asked to pose in front of George's camera: having expired during an inebriated visit to a prostitute, Mr. Hardy, George's father, has been relocated and photographed at his family home as propriety necessitated.

As neither servant nor family, Myrtle's narration is especially revealing: her fluid position within the society of the house reveals Mrs. Hardy's hysterics, the complaints and interests of the servants, Dr. Potter's philosophical musings, and George's character, ethics, and preoccupations. Her episodic observations of Liverpool reflect a place of teeming motives and activities. She sees an accident, an apparent theft and a "Christian act" (18) of recovery, and "ragged boys on the corner . . . wild children squabbling in the gutter" (22) en route to visit the home of a prostitute, her face "distorted with fright" (22), in whose bed George's father died. She observes him naked, surprised at the "limpness of his private parts" after having been exposed to his "thing rigid as a carrot" (26) years before. Myrtle's seeming motto—"It was of no interest to me where I came from, only where I was going" (21)—encourages her to assist George and a street urchin she names "duck-boy" to return the corpse to its bed at the Hardy home, where it can then be discovered that

George's father passed away in a proper place and manner. Preserved for historical posterity, the Victorian "documentary truth" of "Girl in the Presence of Death," then, is exposed as not only fiction but also a sleight of hand used to preserve the propriety valued by polite society.

Taking place four years later, "Plate 2. 1850 A Veil Lifted" is narrated by Myrtle's "duck-boy," Pompey Jones, who, streetwise and wary, regards George and his privilege with some suspicion. George has been judged "as bookish and of a saintly disposition" (43), but Jones knows otherwise. He states that he "didn't wholeheartedly despise George Hardy," even though he considered him "a hypocrite" (47); the "lack of ease" (48) and distance between the two men, furthermore, is a result of Jones's involvement with the scandalous moving of Mr. Hardy's corpse. Unwilling to work as a servant, Jones makes a living taking photographs and helping George in various capacities, including setting up tableaux and developing photographs. Although the strict focus of "A Veil Lifting" is on Victorian scientific experimentation—George etherizing and later photographing an ape whose cataracts he plans to remove—Bainbridge also examines Jones's perspectives and place in society. For example, conversation reveals Jones's unexpressed affection for Myrtle, who is at boarding school, and his anger about George's blithe lack of awareness that he is the object of Myrtle's love. After the ordeal of surgery, Jones helps George develop his photographic studies of the recuperating ape and later spends time with George, now drunk and philosophical. In the evening he rebuffs George's sexual attention (he states, "I wasn't a stranger to that sort of happening, nor unduly alarmed by it, and if he'd not laid on the flattery I might have indulged him"—homosexuality a "vice" in his view that the wealthy "bend to from inclination" and the poor "more often of necessity" [61]). Jones's day concludes with Dr. Potter's accusation that Jones had been disrespectful of the Hardy family's hospitality and his being banished from their home.

The final four chapters of *Master Georgie* are set in Crimea during 1854. Bainbridge's novel, reflecting the largely uninformed or circumstantial ignorance of the narrators, does not comment directly or in detail on the international political dimensions and effects of the Crimean War (1853–56), except to depict scenes of martial carnage, disarray, and confusion as well as the comic antics and intimate conversations brought on by hardship. Dr. Potter's narration, like that of Dr. Wilson in *The Birthday Boys*, reflects a dispassionate man whose self-absorption, scientific curiosity, and fondness for classical authors and conceits lead him to be regarded by Pompey Jones and Myrtle as pompous, a pedant with a less-than-remarkable awareness of the true ways of the world. Despite the bucolic image evoked by the chapter title, "Plate 3. 1854 Tug-of-War beside the Sweet Waters of Europe," Potter's narration there depicts scenes from the group's "ill-advised excursion to Constantinople" (67). Traveling with Hardy, Myrtle, Jones, Annie, and Beatrice, Potter relates stories about Naughton, an "odious and obsequious" (69) representative of the Liverpool Board of Commerce who becomes attracted to George's "sister" Myrtle. Informed by George that Myrtle is engaged to be married and by Potter that her engagement is to a captain of the Eleventh Hussars, Naughton's resultant behavior leads to mishaps both comic and dire. Potter's various observations—about war profiteering, confusing military news, Lyell's *Principles of Geology*, the surprising adaptability of the women, and the "absurd sight" (81) of dancing dervishes—lead him to conclude that in the "reckless bonhomie" of daily experience in Crimea there is "something of the hectic gaiety which must have prevailed during the last days of Rome" (81). Bainbridge portrays Potter as a dispassionate man of reason and philosophically inclined, appalled by "nauseating display of patriotic fervour" (83), pensive (upon receiving news about the wars) about "whether one considers things personal rather than universal to be of paramount importance" (82), and following an evening at the opera during which Naughton attacks a man he has been led to believe badly mistreated Myrtle, introspective about events being accidental or ordained (90) and about cause and effect (97).

Potter's distress contrasts with Myrtle's calm in "Plate 4. August 1854 Concert Party at Varna." In Myrtle's second section of narration, she reveals that she has "never felt more healthy in [her] life" in this "most beautiful spot" (107). Freed from the strictures of English society, she reveals herself to be more assertive, independent, and opinionated (calling Potter, for example, irritating and fatuous—"If we were sitting in a drawing room among fools I'd be the first to think him clever" (108)—and handling the inquisitive Mrs. Yardley with expertise). Though she maintains worldliness about social exchanges and values, remarking, "Nothing is for free in this world" (113), Myrtle's conflicted and unresolved sentiments about her unrequited love for George and her social status align her with characters such as Freda in *The Bottle Factory Outing* and Marge in *The Dressmaker*.

Over the concluding chapters, "Plate 5. October 1954 Funeral Procession Shadowed by Beatrice" and "Plate 6. November 1854 Smile, Boys, Smile," Bainbridge observes war's devastating effects. Potter's vantage point in "Plate 5" fixes on the brutality of daily experience, dietary restrictions, and comparisons between the area's glorious past as recorded in the *Odyssey* and its terrible present. In his attempt to prevent himself from "being mastered by the impressions of the moment" (151), he contemplates his past. Nevertheless his quarrels with enlisted men and Myrtle illustrate the failure of his resolve and the intellectual distance between him and his fellows. Potter's exposure to disturbing scenes—a shell-shocked horse, a soldier's self-mutilation, a funeral service in a muddy former orchard—are met with warm recollections of his love for Beatrice and acknowledgment of Lyell's supposition that the "human race faced not merely extinction but the gradual obliteration of every trace of its existence" (164).

In the final chapter of *Master Georgie,* Pompey Jones's response to Potter—"He rambles on about medieval times, which I take to be some years in the past" (167)—reinforces the insularity of Potter and the class differences among the three narrators. Jones's subsequent observations of the landscape surrounding Sebastapol, that "bleak gap [that] is apparently the reason for all this misery" (168), emphasizes the gruesome human mayhem and resignedly accepts the arbitrariness of fate:

> There's no telling who will live and who will not. A man can have his limbs torn off, the blood draining out of him like a leaking barrel, and recover; another can stumble in with no more than a flesh wound to the groin and snuff it within twenty-four hours. Those whose stomachs have been ploughed up, their innards dangling like pale links of pork, fare the worst. Neither will-power nor medicine can save them. (170)

His account—describing the deaths of soldiers, conflicts with Potter and George and admitting to attempting physical intimacy with Myrtle (or to make her accept that they "were of a kind" [183])—does not examine the war as a historical event of international consequences. Rather it depicts ordinary thoughts and exchanges during extraordinarily chaotic days. During a bloody siege Pompey reaches Georgie, Myrtle by his side, just in time to witness George being fatally shot by a wounded Russian soldier. Assisting a photographer who wants to capture a "posed group of survivors to show the folks back home" (190), Pompey carries George over his shoulder and props up the corpse with the group in front of the camera. As the photographer urges the men with "Smile, boys, smile," Pompey sees Myrtle in the distance, "circling round and round, like a bird above a robbed nest" (190). Concluding with the death of an eminent Victorian who dies senselessly only to be resurrected in as a patriotic image designed to inspire morale, the complex acts of representation within *Master Georgie*—highlighting the partiality of the views of George, the story's ostensible subject, and the fictiveness of historical artifacts themselves—destabilize any certainty the basic narrative establishes.

Icon Rendering: *According to Queeney*

According to Queeney (2001) is especially remarkable insofar as its setting, England 1765–84, represents the most distant reach of Bainbridge's historical novels.[11] Its ostensible focus is late-eighteenth-century domestic life, in particular that of the well-heeled household of Hester Thrale (whose published reminiscences, such as *Anecdotes of the Late Samuel Johnson* [1786], together with her diaries and correspondence, are second in importance only to Boswell's biographical writings in defining the characteristics and accomplishments of Samuel Johnson), the socially ambitious wife of Henry, a prosperous brewer. Her aspirations to be a patron of the arts involve her in a complicated relationship with Samuel Johnson. As in her own *Young Adolf* or Peter Ackroyd's *Milton in America*, Bainbridge's sixteenth novel portrays from an oblique angle a towering historical figure that general esteem holds up as an influential man; her treatment of an iconic literary figure, by no means hagiographic, shifts attention from his accomplishments and status to his personal habits and tics, internal anxieties and conflicts, and erratic social presence, thereby rendering Johnson as a troubled yet sympathetic figure. Furthermore Bainbridge complicates her historical represen-tation by concluding her chapters with correspondence. Dated 1807 to 1811 and signed either "H. M. Thrale" or "H. M. Keith" (after 1808), the letters are replies written by the once precocious and acerbic daughter of Hester Thrale. Nicknamed Queeney by Johnson and incapable of sharing her mother's "capacity for happiness" (117), she is forced to face "bleak memories" (118) and "years best forgotten" (78) because she has been contacted by Laetitia Hawkins, an aspiring author writing a memoir of Johnson and his social circle. Asked about specific occurrences and personality traits, Thrale's daughter replies, correcting or controlling the shape of the written record.

Reviews were generally favorable. For instance, the *London Review of Books* focused on the complexity of retrieving historical material and figures. Reviewer Susan Eilenberg concluded her lengthy review with apparent puzzlement:

> The museum of improbable wonders, the cabinet of frauds, the life whose inwardness is accessible only through dissection, the death-mask whose making tugs open the dead man's eyelids: in these objects the novel seems to recognize something of itself and through them warns of readerly

credulity. . . . For a work absorbed in an act of radical sympathy with its subjects, the reader's suspension of disbelief must be at last beside the point.[12]

The *Spectator* described the novel as a "beautiful piece of work," a "spare and evocative" examination of its central theme, "the gap between reason and desire," and the *Times Literary Supplement* review noted the perfect "sour-sweet" flavor and distinct characters (a "memorable collection of not-quite-grotesques") within a novel concerned with "disintegration and incompleteness." In the *New York Times Book Review* Thomas Mallon drew attention to the novel's "sharp, offbeat perceptions" and "grotesque comic touches." Though he assessed *According to Queeney* to not be Bainbridge's "finest or most ambitious work," he conceded that "much of what's always been striking and irreducible about her still resides within it."[13]

The novel's portraiture and tableaux, familiar approaches in Bainbridge's canon, feature attentive observation of Johnson and Thrale in a variety of locations and in complicated and frequently discordant relationships against a backdrop in which disease, death, and decay are found in abundance. In fact opening with "Crisis" and concluding with "Dissolution," *According to Queeney* has commonalities with Bainbridge's earlier fiction; in particular its episodic account of Thrale's involvement with Johnson is marked by mordant comedy (which extends to the perpetually squabbling servants of Johnson's household, Mrs. Williams and Mrs. Desmoulins, and Thrale's family and social set); and the depiction of family, community, society, and cosmos is notable for its showcasing of discord, mishaps, and mortality. The portrayal of Johnson is provocative insofar as it effectively largely disregards Johnson's status as one of England's greatest literary figures. Although the narration by no means overlooks his various accomplishments—as poet, essayist, biographer, lexicographer, and preeminent critic of English literature—the focus on the latter part of his life illuminates his eccentric behavior, erratic outbursts, disabling melancholia, conflicted reason, and overall lack of insight and finesse about interpersonal relations, and it acts to resituate Johnson as an individual and member of a small community of relations instead of as a literary figure and nimble intellect. If the portrait diminishes his stature, it also humanizes Johnson.

As with *Young Adolf* and *Watson's Apology*, the setting of *According to Queeney* reflects a world in which death and dissolution are commonplace. Its prologue envisions a scene on the morning of 15 December 1784 (two days after Johnson's death). His housekeeper, Mrs. Desmoulins, "too old, too used to death, to weep" (1), sees Johnson's body leave the home wrapped in a threadbare carpet en route to William Hunter's School of Anatomy. The autopsy and a report on the size and condition of Johnson's body parts take up a dominant portion of the prologue. From that inaugural image of Johnson as inanimate flesh, the novel shifts back to 1765, where Johnson, aged fifty-six, takes pains to stay out late: "Solitary nights were to be feared, for when darkness fell, the mind, like the eye, saw things less clearly than by day and confusions and perversions of the brain manufactured black thoughts" (4). Despite the apparent grimness and his pervasive "out of sorts" moods, Johnson's mind is also excited because of his attraction to the "sparkling eyes" of Hester Thrale, a exemplary embodiment of the "weaker sex" (104). Even so, his sexual excitement, "physical stirrings of an unmistakable nature," leads to him striking his forehead with his fist to "beat away a loathsome descent into sensuality" (8).

Later, after taking opium with his tea, Johnson is responsible for "a most distressing scene" in which he spasms and yells inhumanly, exhorting God to grant him continued use of his understanding; this is followed by "a demented outpouring of self-condemnation" (15–16). The chapter concludes, as do all subsequent ones, with a letter (dated between 1807 and 1811) written by Hester Thrale's daughter Queeney clarifying the nature of scenes and events for Laetitia Hawkins's biographical sketch.

Subsequent chapters, "Reintegrate 1766," "Sweeting 1776–77," and "Yesterday 1774," offer depictions of Hester Thrale's life as wife, mother, and socialite and that of Johnson at home with his quarrelsome servants. The attention Bainbridge pays to incidental matters—including Queeney's chest pustules, Hester Thrale's sickly and dead children (followed by delivery of her eighth child with sounds like "those of a sow caught by the hind leg" [65]), experiments involving dog stomachs cut open and filled with warm milk (83), fly swarms, a "bird putrefying on the path" (99), a legless man, a famed actor's diseased gums, and an idiot child who prompts what Mr. Thrale calls the abundant "horrors of life" (56)—directs readers to a near Hogarthian panorama of London (though like the narrator of *Harriet Said*, Bainbridge exhibits fascination with the odd, weird, and grotesque rather than a need to judge it). These chapters also highlight the "portly figure" (25) of Johnson and his eccentric and often disruptive "idiot" (85) behavior. From his walk, a zigzag progression, to his character—that of a man "beset by demons" (26) because of a "surplus of emotion" (94) that results from "his brain being too large" (100)—Bainbridge is emphatic in her depiction of Johnson's oddity. From highly anxious preoccupation with his imaginary ceaseless indolence to suddenly tearing off his clothing and plunging into a lake, the man appears beset by mania. His perception—"I am not alone . . . the world is full of madmen" (30)—complements that of Hester Thrale, who is watching her dinner party acquaintance Mrs. Jackson encounter the great man for the first time:

> It was obvious that she had not been prepared for an encounter with Mr. Johnson, and though her husband may have explained to her that she was to rub shoulders with the great lexicographer and poet, it was doubtful if he had thought to paint a true portrait. The reality of Johnson, in appearance and behaviour, the scarred skin of his cheeks and neck, his large lips forever champing, his shabby clothing and too small wig with its charred top-piece, his tics and mutterings, his propensity to behave as though no one else was present, was at variance with the elegant demeanour imagined to be proper to a man of genius. (33)

Even after hearing of Hester Thrale's experience of Queeney nearly choking to death, Johnson can only think of his own pains. Despite the seeming harshness of the portrait, Bainbridge does not judge Johnson as a self-absorbed and vicious wit in, for instance, the manner of Joseph Surface in Sheridan's 1777 comedy *The School for Scandal*, but instead as a melancholic and graceless man whose outbursts and zigzags are the result of mental illness. The at once tumultuous and virtually invisible romance between Johnson and Mrs. Thrale, moreover, results in greater upset. Although neither party appears fully cognizant of their romantic attraction, their disputes and agonized separations create further discord and consternation in the households of both.

As the names of the final chapters—"Revolution 1775," "Disaster 1776–77," and "Dissolution 1776–77"—imply, the social network that includes Johnson, the Thrales, and an entourage of polite society aspirants undergoes further strife, hardship, and disharmonious relations. The chapters capture the extreme vicissitudes of the life of the social grouping—a trip to France that reflects the regained fortune of the Thrale brewery followed by the sudden death of the Thrale son and the mania and fatal eating disorder of Henry Thrale. Even a leisurely trip to France following the sixty-sixth birthday of Johnson and the eleventh of Henrietta is not without conflict. When Johnson grows weary of the group's enthusiasm over sights, he becomes irritable, difficult, and quarrelsome; his self-absorption, moreover, creates hostility with the Thrales even though Hester justifies his behavior as characteristic of a man who "lived in the head rather than the body" (127). Hester Thrale's "vexations" (130) stem from group dynamics, Johnson's contrary comments (as well as her efforts to shore up his sanity), and her family, whereas Johnson's come from his numerous personal demons and "moods" (139). Incidents such as Johnson's being "not himself" after witnessing an act of buggery in a cellar (144) and being perceived to lose his mind (145) in a village named Lille lead to further distance between himself and Hester Thrale. Seeing his continued selfishness and what Hester considers weakness of resolve (following his failure to consummate their relationship), Johnson's benefactor concludes, "It was curious, was it not, that great men who compiled dictionaries, whose intellect enabled them to expound upon the states of nations, had not the words or the understanding to define the small business of love" (164).

"Dissolution," the novel's final chapter, reveals the steady decay of the Thrale marriage, which results from mutual infatuations, Henry Thrale's stroke, a stillborn child, quarrels between various members of the Thrale social circle, and Henry's ignoble death from ruptured lungs ("He uttered no last words, merely let forth a prolonged expulsion of wind" [197]). Hester Thrale withdraws from Johnson because of his irascible nature and her personal tragedies. He, in turn, expresses extreme anguish and anger at her failings. Upon hearing of her eventual descent into madness and death, Johnson asks, "Did she dwell on me?" and soon feels "recovered in health" (211) with daily usage of opium. The autopsy of Johnson's body opens the novel, and the epilogue revisits the day, viewing the funeral procession and the lowering of his coffin into the ground at Westminster Abbey. The final image of the novel focuses on Mrs. Desmoulins, alone, roasting chestnuts at the fire. Death, dissolution, and uncertainty, mainstays of Bainbridge's fiction since her juvenile short stories written in 1945, encourage an understanding of Johnson and Thrale and their era that emphasizes achievement and historical stature less than pained subjectivity, fragile mortality, and difficult social intercourse in a distant world whose topography is impossible to fully comprehend.

Notes

Chapter 1—Understanding Beryl Bainbridge

1. Beryl Bainbridge, "How I Began," in *Collected Stories*, by Beryl Bainbridge (London: Penguin, 1994), 2.

2. Bainbridge, *English Journey, or The Road to Milton Keynes* (New York: Carroll and Graf, 1997), 88.

3. In the introduction to *Front Row* (London: Continuum, 2005), Bainbridge reminisces about the "far-off days" when she learned elocution, ballet dancing, and stagecraft (1–8).

4. Bainbridge, *English Journey*, 89. Also see Shusha Guppy's interview, "Beryl Bainbridge: The Art of Fiction CLXIV," *Paris Review* 157 (Winter 2000): 242–68.

5. In Clare Boylan, ed., *The Agony and the Ego: The Art and Strategy of Fiction Writing Explored* (London: Penguin, 1993), Bainbridge discusses her ambivalent relationship with her occupation: "Sometimes I think of getting a job and then sneaking home in the evenings to write. I live like a recluse. You can't share a bed with anyone if you're going to read aloud all night. I avoid quarrels because they make me miserable and then I can't work, so it means that vital issues in relationships never get confronted. Most of the time I wonder what it's all for. It's a mug's game. It's no way for a normal person to live" (256).

6. Ibid., 84.

7. Guppy, "Beryl Bainbridge," 249.

8. Ibid., 99–100.

9. Ibid., 7.

10. Ibid., 99.

11. Ibid., 85.

12. Ibid., 85, 86.

13. Ibid., 85; Bainbridge, "How I Began," 2. See Bainbridge's introduction to *Forever England: North and South* (London: Duckworth, 1987) for an additional representation of her father.

14. Bainbridge, *English Journey*, 7.

15. Bainbridge, "How I Began," 1.

16. Ibid.

17. Bainbridge, *English Journey*, 7.

18. Frank Kermode, "Coming Up for Air," *New York Review of Books,* 15 July 1976, 42.

19. Elisabeth Wennö, *Ironic Formula in the Novels of Beryl Bainbridge* (Göteborg: Acta Universitatis Gothoburgensis, 1993), x, 3, iv, 8, 1.

20. John F. Baker, "Beryl Bainbridge," in *Writing for Your Life #4,* ed. Jonathan Bing (Wainscott, N.Y: Pushcart Press, 2000), 6.

21. Nick Rennison, *Contemporary British Novelists* (London: Routledge, 2005), 17.

22. Rennison likewise points out that such "neat compartmentalization" can create a misleading impression about the development of her fiction (ibid., 14–15).

23. Malcolm Bradbury, *The Modern British Novel* (London: Secker and Warburg, 1993), 388. In comparison, in *The Hidden Script: Writing and the Unconscious* (London: Routledge and Kegan Paul, 1985), David Punter observes in Bainbridge the inclination to destroy rather than chronicle: "Thus there is in Bainbridge a wish for rebellion, but no special interest in the rebel: the excitement is more pure than that, more focused on downfall and the upturning of a deadly world." Punter, *The Hidden Script: Writing and the Unconscious* (London: Routledge and Kegan Paul, 1985), 60.

24. Dominic Head, *The Cambridge Introduction to Modern British Fiction, 1950–2000* (London: Cambridge University Press, 2002), 3, 2.

25. Bradbury, *Modern British Novel,* 388; Rennison, *Contemporary British Novelists,* 17; Peter Ackroyd, *Albion: The Origins of the English Imagination* (London: Chatto and Windus, 2002), 279.

26. Louis Kronenberger, *The Thread of Laughter* (New York: Knopf, 1952), 4.

27. Bainbridge, "How I Began," 2.

28. Bainbridge, *English Journey*, 39.

29. And it continues: Victoria Richter, in "Grey Gothic: The Novels of Beryl Bainbridge," *Anglistik und Englischunterricht* 60 (1997): 159–71, reads Bainbridge's work as neo-Gothic and identifies "her very special treatment of 'horror'" (159) as a key characteristic.

30. Patrick O'Neill, *The Comedy of Entropy: Humour/Narrative/Reading* (Toronto: University of Toronto Press, 1990), 50.

31. Christopher Herbert, "Comedy: The World of Pleasure," *Genre* 17 (Winter 1984): 402, 401. See also *The Idea of Comedy: History, Theory, Critique* (Madison, N.J.: Fairleigh Dickinson University Press, 2006), in which Jan Walsh Hokenson states that "each cultural era in the West has contributed some theoretical perspective, or revised the received idea of comedy in some significant way or another, steadily amplifying our idea of the comic. The theoretical texts are extensive. They are also increasingly disputatious, often asserting contradictory interpretations and clashing, even diametrically opposed claims about the aims and means of comedy" (13).

32. O'Neill, *Comedy of Entropy*, 8, 22. O'Neill notes that in the "continuum of humour" it stands oppositional to the renewing "humour of order" (52).

33. Alice Rayner, *Comic Persuasion: Moral Structure in British Comedy from Shakespeare to Stoppard* (Berkeley and Los Angeles: University of California Press, 1987), 13.

34. Ibid.

35. Bainbridge, *English Journey*, 84.

36. Bainbridge, *Collected Stories*, 197.

37. Baker, "Beryl Bainbridge," 2.

38. Ibid., 4.

39. Avrom Fleishman, *The English Historical Novel: Walter Scott to Virginia Woolf* (Baltimore: Johns Hopkins University Press, 1971), 4.

40. Ibid.

41. Beryl Bainbridge, *Watson's Apology* (New York: Carroll and Graf, 2001), 6.

42. Margaret Scanlan, *Traces of Another Time: History and Politics in Postwar British Fiction* (Princeton: Princeton University Press, 1990), 12. Scanlan later offers an encapsulation: "History as presented in the contemporary British novel is neither glamorous nor consoling. It is too diffuse to offer lessons, too unfinished to constitute a space into which we can escape; and we ourselves, implicated in the failures of the past, cannot even enjoy its ironies comfortably. Whatever the authors' professed politics, their novels resonate with a profound pessimism about the consequences of public action. What actuates these fictions is not, then, a confidence that the past will teach us how to behave, but a quieter conviction that it is better to know than to remain ignorant, even though what we learn is the enormous difficulty of understanding our lives historically" (16).

43. Ibid., 10.

Chapter 2—Opening Strategies

1. In her overview of Bainbridge, Barbara C. Millard notes that the author describes *Another Part of the Wood* as hastily written as well as a reaction to the breakup of her marriage and an attempt to impress her former husband; she dismisses the experimental narrative style of *A Weekend with Claud* as "impossible . . . it just goes on and on." Millard, "Beryl Bainbridge," in *British Novelists since 1960*, ed. Jay L. Halio, Dictionary of Literary Biography 14 (Detroit: Gale, 1983), 41.

2. John Richetti, ed., *The Columbia History of the British Novel* (New York: Columbia University Press, 1994), xii.

3. David Punter, *The Hidden Script: Writing and the Unconscious* (London: Routledge and Kegan Paul, 1985) 60.

4. Patrick O'Neill, *The Comedy of Entropy: Humour/Narrative/Reading* (Toronto: University of Toronto Press, 1990), 143.

5. Bainbridge, *A Weekend with Claud* (London: Hutchinson, 1967); revised as *A Weekend with Claude* (London: Duckworth, 1981); page references, indicated in the text parenthetically, are to the 1981 Duckworth edition. See Gloria Valverde's 1985 Texas Tech

University dissertation, "A Textual Study of Beryl Bainbridge's *Another Part of the Wood* and *A Weekend with Claude*," for an in-depth discussion of the differences. In general, Valverde argues that the revised versions of both novels are notable for what the author deleted (scenes, descriptions, explanations and characterization, didactic passages).

6. Unsigned review of *A Weekend with Claud*, by Beryl Bainbridge, *Times Literary Supplement*, 6 July 1967, 604; Karl Miller, "A Novelist Worth Knowing," *New York Review of Books*, 16 May 1974, 25; J. D. S. Haworth, "Fiction: Printers' Devil," *Listener*, 20 July 1967, 89.

7. In addition to reducing the size of the novel by fifty pages, Bainbridge changed the name of one of the narrators. "Maggie," the first titled section in the 1967 edition, becomes "Lily."

8. Bainbridge, *Another Part of the Wood* (London: Hutchinson, 1968; revised, London: Duckworth, 1981); page references, indicated in the text parenthetically, are to the 1980 paperback edition published in London by Duckworth.

9. Emma Fisher, review of *Another Part of the Wood*, by Beryl Bainbridge, *Spectator*, 8 December 1979, 25; John Naughton, "Creepies," *Listener*, 13 December 1979, 825; Miller, "A Novelist Worth Knowing," 26.

10. O'Neill, *Comedy of Entropy*, 65.

11. Bainbridge, *Harriet Said* (London: Duckworth, 1972; New York: Braziller, 1973); page references, indicated in the text parenthetically, are to the 1972 Duckworth edition. In her interview with Guppy, Bainbridge tartly recalls, "Nobody wanted to touch it; they said it was obscene, peculiar" ("Beryl Bainbridge," 254).

12. Gail Godwin, review of *Harriet Said*, *New York Times Book Review*, 30 September 1973, 39; Auberon Waugh, "Young Pretenders," *Spectator*, 14 October 1972, 584; "The Tsar Next Door," unsigned review of *Harriet Said*, by Beryl Bainbridge, *Times Literary Supplement*, 6 October 1972, 1184; Miller, "A Novelist Worth Knowing," 27.

13. Barbara C. Millard, "Beryl Bainbridge," in *British Novelists since 1960*, ed. Jay L. Halio, Dictionary of Literary Biography 14 (Detroit: Gale, 1983), 41.

14. Punter, for instance, concludes his psychological reading of the gender dynamics of the novel with the following summation: "Thus is depicted the fate of an entire culture, starved of meaning . . . and thus trapped into a murderous resentment of change (*Hidden Script*, 66).

15. Elisabeth Wennö, *Ironic Formula in the Novels of Beryl Bainbridge* (Göteborg: Acta Universitatis Gothoburgensis, 1993), 139.

16. Ibid., 154.

Chapter 3—Perilous Aspirations

1. Both novels were originally published in London by Duckworth, *The Dressmaker* in 1973, *The Bottle Factory Outing* in 1974; references indicated parenthetically in the text are to the paperback editions published in London by Penguin (1992) and by Fontana (1975), respectively. In her interview with Guppy, Bainbridge describes *The Dressmaker* as being "about my two aunts" and *The Bottle Factory Outing* as reflecting her experience as a worker in such a factory (stating that "the story was all true, apart from the murder plot") ("Beryl Bainbridge," 254–56).

2. In *Ironic Formula in the Novels of Beryl Bainbridge* (Göteborg: Acta Universitatis Gothoburgensis, 1993), Elisabeth Wennö discusses the novel's conflict as a dichotomy between culture and nature (96–110), concluding that the conflict between nature and culture remains unresolved: the "women remain where they always were, united only by their shared predicament of being in the futile pursuit of an ideal (nature-culture harmony, or death-life transcendence) that never materializes" (110).

3. "Bad Old Days," unsigned review of *The Dressmaker*, by Beryl Bainbridge, *Times Literary Supplement*, 28 September 1973, 1101; Karl Miller, "A Novelist Worth Knowing," *New York Review of*

Books, 16 May 1974, 28; Elaine Feinstein, "Numbness," *Listener,* 27 September 1973, 426; Gerald Weales, review of *The Dressmaker,* by Beryl Bainbridge, *New Republic,* 28 September 1974, 27–28; Phoebe Adams, review of *The Dressmaker,* by Beryl Bainbridge, *Atlantic,* September 1974, 103.

4. David Punter, *The Hidden Script: Writing and the Unconscious* (London: Routledge and Kegan Paul, 1985), 65.

5. Krystyna Stamirowska, "The Bustle and Crudity of Life: The Novels of Beryl Bainbridge," *Kwartalnik Neofilologiczny* 35, no. 4 (1988): 450.

6. Wennö's discussion of the novel focuses on the "discrepancy between the ideal and the actual," which "serves the function of exposing the attainability of perfection as an illusion, but also, as we have seen, of pointing to human potentials and values that are lost or misused, but, by implication, attainable" (*Ironic Formula,* 162). She does not comment on the comic aspect.

7. Susannah Clapp, "Rewards of Embarrassment," *Times Literary Supplement,* 1 November 1974, 1217; Peter Ackroyd, "This England," *Spectator,* 2 November 1974, 573; Guy Davenport, "Two English Comedies, One That Works," *New York Times Book Review,* 8 June 1975, 6; Lynne Sharon Schwartz, review of *The Bottle Factory Outing,* by Beryl Bainbridge, *New Republic,* 24 May 1975, 26, 27, 27.

8. Dominic Head's overview of the novel emphasizes its farcical rendering of "cultural misrecognition" (*The Cambridge Introduction to Modern British Fiction, 1950–2000* [London: Cambridge University Press, 2002], 162), and although acknowledging the "Ortonesque business" that concludes the novel, he also notes sobriety: "The despairing undertow of Bainbridge's farce is the clear implication that the popular forces of English social change have a long way to go to advance the cause of ethnic integration" (163).

9. Stamirowska, "Bustle and Crudity," 455.

10. Punter, *Hidden Script,* 67.

Chapter 4—Domestic Lives

1. All three novels were originally published in London by Duckworth: *Sweet William* in 1975, *A Quiet Life* in 1976, and *Injury Time* in 1977; references indicated parenthetically in the text are to the paperback editions published in London by Fontana (1976), Fontana (1977), and Abacus (2003), respectively.

2. Peter Tinniswood, review of *A Quiet Life*, by Beryl Bainbridge, *London Times*, 30 September 1976.

3. Frank Kermode, "Coming Up for Air," *New York Review of Books*, 15 July 1976, 42, 43, 43, 43; John Mellors, "Midlands Money," *Listener*, 9 October 1975, 486; Susannah Clapp, "Goings-on in North London," *Times Literary Supplement*, 3 October 1975, 112; Katha Pollitt, review of *Sweet William*, *New York Times Book Review*, 16 May 1976, 5, 5, 6, 6.

4. David Punter views the fragmented or split female self as a characteristic theme in Bainbridge's fiction. Punter, *The Hidden Script: Writing and the Unconscious* (London: Routledge and Kegan Paul, 1985), 69.

5. In *Ironic Formula in the Novels of Beryl Bainbridge* (Göteborg: Acta Universitatis Gothoburgensis, 1993), Elisabeth Wennö comments that what "seems to be a simple and rather banal love story of the victimization of woman by philandering man" (122) can also be understood as a meditation about the falsity of love and union as means of transcendence and the idea of "separation as truth" (132).

6. Krystyna Stamirowska, "The Bustle and Crudity of Life: The Novels of Beryl Bainbridge," *Kwartalnik Neofilologiczny* 35, no. 4 (1988): 449.

7. Punter, *Hidden Script*, 70.

8. Francis Wyndham, "Compression Chamber, *Times Literary Supplement*, 8 October 1976, 1268; Julia O'Faolain, "Getting Away with Murder," *New York Times Book Review*, 20 March 1977, 6; John Mellors, "Unreasonable Men," *Listener*, 21 October 1976, 518.

9. Wennö, *Ironic Formula*, 171.

10. Punter, *Hidden Script*, 74.

11. A. L. Barker, "No Pudding," *The Listener*, 29 September 1977, 409, 409, 410; Michael Wood, "Nothing Sacred," *New York Review of Books*, 20 April 1978, 9, 9, 9, 11, 11, 11, 11, 12; Katha Pollitt, "A Messy Affair," *New York Times Book Review,* 26 February 1978, 15.

Chapter 5—Closures and Transitions

1. Bainbridge, *Forever England: North and South* (London: Duckworth, 1987), 9.

2. Barbara C. Millard, "Beryl Bainbridge," in *British Novelists since 1960*, ed. Jay L. Halio, Dictionary of Literary Biography 14 (Detroit: Gale, 1983), 45.

3. Ibid.

4. Beryl Bainbridge, *Young Adolf* (London: Duckworth, 1978). References, hereafter made parenthetically in text, are to the 1979 paperback edition published in London by Fontana.

5. Bainbridge, *English Journey, or The Road to Milton Keynes* (New York: Carroll and Graf, 1997), 7; Beryl Bainbridge, *Something Happened Yesterday* (London: Duckworth, 1993), 7. She states, furthermore, "The authoritarian voice is not for me. I'm not bothered with causes or hard facts; my preoccupation is not with the immediate how and why of the lives we lead, but rather with a raking over of the life we once knew."

6. Bainbridge, *Forever England*, 9.

7. Ibid., 10.

8. Neal Ascherson, "The Damned," *New York Review of Books*, 5 April 1979, 27; John Naughton, "Leavisites in Yorkshire," *Listener*, 16 November 1978, 659; Paul Ableman, "Anti-hero," *Spectator* 11 November 1978, 27; E. S. Shaffer, "Hitler at Heathrow," *London Review of Books,* 7 August 1980, 15; Diane Johnson, "The Sufferings of Young Hitler," *Times Literary Supplement,* 1 December 1978, 1385.

9. In *Ironic Formula in the Novels of Beryl Bainbridge* (Göteborg: Acta Universitatis Gothoburgensis, 1993), Elisabeth Wennö points out that since from her perspective the novel dramatizes the conflict between the desire to escape from and conform to the conditions of life and concludes envisioning only the impossibility of integration (119), the novel's ostensible focus on Adolf Hitler can also be "read as signifying contexts other than the implied historical context" (111).

10. Phyllis Lassner, calling the novel "Chaplinesque farce," suggests Bainbridge parodies "the Nazi campaign to dehumanize 'the other' by submitting the future Führer to the same fate and exposing England's prevailing social discordances." Lassner, "Between the Gaps: Class and Anarchy in the British Comic Novel of World War II," in *Look Who's Laughing: Gender and Comedy*, ed. Gail Finney (Langhorne, Pa.: Gordon and Breach, 1994), 206.

11. David Punter does not interpret the novel as comic but views it as a kind of psychological allegory illustrating how the roots of fascism are intimately tied to the "inevitable subjugation" of selfhood. Punter, *The Hidden Script: Writing and the Unconscious* (London: Routledge and Kegan Paul, 1985), 75.

12. Beryl Bainbridge, *Winter Garden* (London: Duckworth, 1980; New York: Braziller, 1981); references, hereafter made parenthetically in text, are to the Braziller edition.

13. Paul Ableman, "Fancy-free," *Spectator*, 1 November 1980, 24; Valerie Brooks, "Beryl Bainbridge and Her Tenth Novel," *New York Times Book Review*, 1 March 1981, 9; Anne Duchene, "The Russian Outing," *Times Literary Supplement*, 31 October 1980, 1221; Peter Conrad. "Losing It All," *Listener*, 20 November 1980, 700.

14. Patrick O'Neill, *The Comedy of Entropy: Humour/Narrative/Reading* (Toronto: University of Toronto Press, 1990), 8.

15. *Watson's Apology* was originally published in London by Duckworth, 1984. References in this book, hereafter made parenthetically in text, are to the 2001 paperback edition published by in New York by Carroll and Graf.

16. Avrom Fleishman, *The English Historical Novel: Walter Scott to Virginia Woolf* (Baltimore: Johns Hopkins University Press, 1971), 4.

17. Humphrey Carpenter, "Kiss Me, Hardy," *London Review of Books,* 15 November 1984, 23; Ronald Blythe, "Marriage and Murder, *Listener,* 25 October 1984, 23; Marilyn Stasio, "He Did, She Howled," *New York Times Book Review,* 20 October 1985, 7, 9, 7, 9.

18. Beryl Bainbridge, *An Awfully Big Adventure* (London: Duckworth, 1989). References in this chapter, hereafter made parenthetically in text, are to the 1993 paperback edition published in New York by Carroll and Graf.

19. Lindsay Duguid, "The Lost Children of the Props-room," *Times Literary Supplement,* 15 December 1989, 1385; Peter Parker, "Straight On to Mourning," *Listener,* 11 January 1990, 25; Peter Campbell, "People Who Love People Who Love Somebody Else," *London Review of Books,* 25 January 1990, 19.

Chapter 6—Fictions of History

The epigraph is from Laurie Taylor, "That's for the Fellahs," *New Humanist* 119 (January–February 2004), http://newhumanist.org .uk/691 (accessed 15 January 2008).

1. Frederick M. Holmes, *The Historical Imagination: Postmodernism and the Treatment of the Past in Contemporary British Fiction,* English Literary Studies Monograph Series 73 (Victoria, B.C.: University of Victoria, 1997), 11.

2. *The Birthday Boys* was originally published in London by Duckworth in 1991. References in this chapter, hereafter made parenthetically in text, are to the 1993 paperback edition published in London by Penguin.

3. Andro Linklater, "No Longer Hero or Villain," *Spectator,* 4 January 1992, 25–26; Gary Krist, "Antarctic Antics," *New York Times Book Review,* 17 April 1994, 15; D. J. Enright, "Just Going Outside," *London Review of Books,* 30 January 1992, 16; Francis

Spufford, "In Scott's Footsteps," *Times Literary Supplement*, 20 December 1991, 24.

4. *Every Man for Himself* was originally published in London by Duckworth in 1996. References in this chapter, hereafter made parenthetically in text, are to the American paperback edition published in New York in 1997 by Carroll and Graf.

5. Kenneth Womack, "Reading the *Titanic*: Contemporary Literary Representations of the Ship of Dreams," *Interdisciplinary Literary Studies* 5 (Fall 2003): 35.

6. Gabriele Annan, "Only the Drop," *London Review of Books,* 17 October 1996, 16; Jonathan Keates, "Going Down with the Unsinkable," *Times Literary Supplement,* 6 September 1996, 21; John Updike, "It Was Sad," *New Yorker,* 14 October 1996, 98, 97; Jane Gardam, "It Was Sad When the Great Ship Went Down," *Spectator,* 14 September 1996, 35; Janet Kaye, "A Night to Remember," *New York Times Book Review*, 22 December 1996, 21.

7. *Master Georgie* was originally published in London by Duckworth in 1998. References in this chapter, hereafter made parenthetically in text, are to the American edition published in New York in 1998 by Carroll and Graf.

8. Linda Hutcheon, *A Poetics of Postmodernism: History, Theory, Fiction* (New York: Routledge, 1988), 111.

9. Ana María Sánchez-Arce, "The Prop They Need: Undressing and the Politics of War in Beryl Bainbridge's *Master Georgie*," in *Dressing Up for War: Transformations of Gender and Genre in the Discourse and Literature of War,* ed. Aránzazu Usandizaga and Andrew Monnickendam, Rodopi Perspectives on Modern Literature 24 (Amsterdam and New York: Rodopi, 2001): 93.

10. Sarah Rigby, "Mind's Eye," *London Review of Books,* 7 August 1980, 27; Francine Prose, "Expiration Dates," *New York Times Book Review,* 29 November 1998, 5; James Michie, "By Delayed Exposure," *Spectator*, 25 April 1988, 38; David Horspool, "In the Fog of Battle," *Times Literary Supplement,* 24 April 1998, 22.

11. *According to Queeney* was originally published in London by Little, Brown in 2001. References in this chapter, made parenthetically in text, are to the American paperback edition published in New York in 2002 by Carroll and Graf.

12. Susan Eilenberg, "Leaf, Button, Dog," *London Review of Books,* 1 November 2001, 15–17.

13. Salley Vickers, "Agonistes," *Spectator,* 18 August 2001, 36; Henry Hitchings, "A Desperate Fragility," *Times Literary Supplement,* 7 September 2001, 3; Thomas Mallon, "The Man Who Came to Dinner," *New York Times Book Review,* 12 August 2001, 9.

Bibliography

Works by Beryl Bainbridge

Novels

A Weekend with Claud. London: Hutchinson, 1967. (Revised edition published as *A Weekend with Claude*. London: Duckworth, 1981; New York: Braziller, 1982.)

Another Part of the Wood. London: Hutchinson, 1968. (Revised edition, London: Duckworth, 1981; New York: Braziller, 1980.)

Harriet Said. London: Duckworth, 1972; New York: Braziller, 1973.

The Dressmaker. London: Duckworth, 1973. (Republished as *The Secret Glass*. New York: Braziller, 1973.)

The Bottle Factory Outing. London: Duckworth, 1974; New York: Braziller, 1975.

Sweet William. London: Duckworth, 1975; New York: Braziller, 1976.

A Quiet Life. London: Duckworth, 1976; New York: Braziller, 1977.

Injury Time. London: Duckworth, 1977; New York: Braziller, 1977.

Young Adolf. London: Duckworth, 1978; New York: Braziller, 1979.

Winter Garden. London: Duckworth, 1980; New York: Braziller, 1981.

English Journey, or The Road to Milton Keynes. London: Duckworth, 1984; New York: Braziller, 1984.

Watson's Apology. London: Duckworth, 1984; New York: McGraw-Hill, 1985.

Mum and Mr. Armitage. London: Duckworth, 1985; New York: McGraw-Hill, 1987.

Filthy Lucre, or The Tragedy of Ernest Ledwhistle and Richard Soleway. London: Duckworth: 1986.

Forever England: North and South. London: Duckworth, 1987.

An Awfully Big Adventure. London: Duckworth, 1989; New York: HarperCollins, 1991.

The Birthday Boys. London: Duckworth, 1991; New York: Carroll and Graf, 1996.

Something Happened Yesterday. London: Duckworth, 1993.

Collected Stories. London: Penguin, 1994.

"Mr. Chips." In *Colin Haycraft, 1929–1994: Maverick Publisher*, edited by Stoddard Martin, 51–55. London: Duckworth, 1995.

Every Man for Himself. London: Duckworth, 1996; New York: Carroll and Graf, 1996.

Master Georgie. London: Duckworth, 1998; New York: Carroll and Graf, 1998.

According to Queeney. London: Little, Brown, 2001; New York: Carroll and Graf, 2001.

Front Row: Evenings at the Theatre. London: Continuum, 2005.

Volumes Edited

New Stories 6. London: Hutchinson, 1981.

Television Scripts (Produced by the BBC)

Tiptoe through the Tulips. 1976.

Blue Skies from Now On. 1977.

It's a Lovely Day Tomorrow. 1977.

The Warrior's Return. 1977.

Sweet William. 1979.

Words Fail Me. 1979.

The Journal of Bridget Hitler. 1980. With Phillip Seville.

A Quiet Life. 1980.

Somewhere More Central. 1981.

Evensong. 1986.

Works about Beryl Bainbridge

Selected Reviews of Novels

Ableman, Paul. "Anti-hero." *Spectator*, 11 November 1978, 23–24.

———. "Fancy-free." *Spectator*, 1 November 1980, 24.

Ackroyd, Peter. "This England." *Spectator*, 2 November 1974, 573.

Annan, Gabriele. "Only the Drop." *London Review of Books*, 17 October 1996, 16.

Ascherson, Neal. "The Damned." *New York Review of Books*, 5 April 1979, 27–28.

"Bad Old Days." *Times Literary Supplement*, 28 September 1973, 1101.

Barker, A. L. "No Pudding." *Listener*, 29 September 1977, 409–10.

Blythe, Ronald. "Marriage and Murder." *Listener*, 25 October 1984, 23.

Brookner, Anita. "Nostalgia for Something Awful." *Spectator*, 9 December 1972, 37.

Brooks, Valerie. "Beryl Bainbridge and Her Tenth Novel." *New York Times Book Review*, 1 March 1981, 9, 27.

Campbell, Peter. "People Who Love People Who Love Somebody Else." *London Review of Books*, 25 January 1990, 19–20.

Carpenter, Humphrey. "Kiss Me, Hardy." *London Review of Books*, 15 November 1984, 23.

Clapp, Susannah. "Goings-on in North London." *Times Literary Supplement*, 3 October 1975, 1125.

———. "Rewards of Embarrassment." *Times Literary Supplement*, 1 November 1974, 1217.

Conrad, Peter. "Losing It All." *Listener*, 20 November 1980, 699–700.

Duchene, Anne. "The Russian Outing." *Times Literary Supplement*, 31 October 1980, 1221.

Duguid, Lindsay. "The Lost Children of the Props-room." *Times Literary Supplement*, 15 December 1989, 1385.

Eilenberg, Susan. "Leaf, Button, Dog." *London Review of Books*, 1 November 2001, 15–17.

Enright, D. J. "Just Going Outside." *London Review of Books*, 30 January 1992, 16.

Feinstein, Elaine. "Numbness." *Listener*, 27 September 1973, 426.

Fisher, Emma. Review of *Another Part of the Wood*. *Spectator*, 8 December 1979, 25–26.

Gardam, Jane. "It Was Sad When the Great Ship Went Down." *Spectator*, 14 September 1996, 35.

Godwin, Gail. Review of *Harriet Said*. *New York Times Book Review*, 30 September 1973, 38–39.

Hitchings, Henry. "A Desperate Fragility." *Times Literary Supplement*, 7 September 2001, 3.

Horspool, David. "In the Fog of Battle." *Times Literary Supplement*, 24 April 1998, 22.

Johnson, Diane. "The Sufferings of Young Hitler." *Times Literary Supplement*, 1 December 1978, 1385.

Kaye, Janet. "A Night to Remember." *New York Times Book Review*, 22 December 1996, 8.

Keates, Jonathan. "Going Down with the Unsinkable." *Times Literary Supplement*, 6 September 1996, 21.

Kermode, Frank. "Coming Up for Air." *New York Review of Books*, 15 July 1976, 42–44.

Krist, Gary. "Antarctic Antics." *New York Times Book Review*, 17 April 1994, 15.

Linklater, Andro. "No Longer Hero or Villain." *Spectator*, 4 January 1992, 25–26.

Mallon, Thomas. "The Man Who Came to Dinner." *New York Times Book Review*, 12 August 2001, 9.

Mellors, John. "Unreasonable Men." *Listener*, 21 October 1976, 518.

Miller, Karl. "A Novelist Worth Knowing." *New York Review of Books*, 16 May 1974, 25–28.

Naughton, John. "Leavisites in Yorkshire." *Listener*, 16 November 1978, 659.

Parker, Peter. "Straight On till Mourning." *Listener*, 11 January 1990, 25.

Pollitt, Katha. "A Messy Affair." *New York Times Book Review*, 26 February 1978, 15.

Prose, Francine. "Expiration Dates." *New York Times Book Review*, 29 November 1998, 5.

Rigby, Sarah. "Mind's Eye." *London Review of Books*, 4 June 1998, 27–28.

Shaffer, E. E. "Hitler at Heathrow." *London Review of Books*, 7 August 1980, 14–15.

Spufford, Francis. "In Scott's Footsteps." *Times Literary Supplement*, 20 December 1991, 24.

Updike, John. "It Was Sad." *New Yorker*, 14 October 1996, 94–98.

Vickers, Salley. "Agonistes." *Spectator*, 18 August 2001, 36.

Waugh, Auberon. "Young Pretenders." *Spectator*, 14 October 1972, 584.

Wood, Michael. "Nothing Sacred." *New York Review of Books*, 20 April 1978, 9–12.

Wyndham, Francis. "Compression Chamber." *Times Literary Supplement*, 8 October 1976, 1268.

Selected Critical Works

Hutcheon, Linda. *A Poetics of Postmodernism: History, Theory, Fiction*. New York: Routledge, 1988.

Punter, David. *The Hidden Script: Writing and the Unconscious*. London: Routledge and Kegan Paul, 1985. Features a one-chapter discussion of Bainbridge's novels from the 1970s that is shaped by the psychological theories of Lacan and the philosophy of Derrida.

Richter, Virginia. "Grey Gothic: The Novels of Beryl Bainbridge." *Anglistik und Englischunterricht* 60 (1997): 159–71. Characterizes Bainbridge's fiction as neo-Gothic and concerned with the failure and annihilation of the individual.

Stamirowska, Krystyna. "The Bustle and Crudity of Life: The Novels of Beryl Bainbridge." *Kwartalnik Neofilologiczny* 35, no. 4 (1988): 445–56. An overview of *The Dressmaker*, *The Bottle Factory Outing*, and *Sweet William* that focuses on Bainbridge's interest in the interplay of the ordinary, the tragic, and the grotesque.

Valverde, Gloria. "A Textual Study of Beryl Bainbridge's *Another Part of the Wood* and *A Weekend with Claude*." Ph.D. diss., Texas Tech University, 1985. An exhaustive comparison of the changes Bainbridge made to each novel when she revised it for republication.

Wennö, Elisabeth. *Ironic Formula in the Novels of Beryl Bainbridge.* Göteborg: Acta Universitatis Gothoburgensis, 1993. A thorough structuralist analysis of Bainbridge's fiction that explicates the roles irony plays in the author's representation of individuality and social relations.

Selected Interviews and Profiles

Baker, John F. "Beryl Bainbridge: Total Immersion in the Past." *Publishers Weekly*, 9 November 1998, 52–53. (Reprinted as "Beryl Bainbridge." In *Writing for Your Life #4*, edited by Jonathan Bing, 1–6. Wainscott, N.Y: Pushcart Press, 2000.)

Bannon, Barbara. "Beryl Bainbridge." *Publishers Weekly*, 15 March 1976, 6–7.

Barber, Lynn. "Beryl's Perils." *Observer*, 19 August 2001, http://observer.guardian.co.uk/life/story/0,,538841,00.html (accessed 15 January 2008).

Brockes, Emma. "Under Her Skin." *Guardian*, 3 October 2005, http://books.guardian.co.uk/departments/generalfiction/story/0,,1583445,00.html (accessed 15 January 2008).

Guppy, Shusha. "Beryl Bainbridge: The Art of Fiction CLXIV." *Paris Review* 157 (Winter 2000): 242–68.

Hamilton, Alex. "Interview with Beryl Bainbridge." *Guardian*, 29 November 1974, 12.

Jones, Victoria. "A Day in the Life of Beryl Bainbridge." *Sunday Times Magazine*, 7 August 1983, 54.

Kinson, Sarah. "Beryl Bainbridge." *Guardian*, 5 March 2007, http://books.guardian.co.uk/whyiwrite/story/0,,2027007,00.html (accessed 15 January 2008).

May, Yolanta. "Beryl Bainbridge Talks to Yolanta May." *New Review* 3, no. 33 (1976): 48–52.

Petschek, Willa. "Beryl Bainbridge and Her Tenth Novel." *New York Times Book Review,* 1 March 1981, 9, 27.

Taylor, Laurie. "That's for the Fellahs." *New Humanist* 119 (January–February 2004), http://newhumanist.org.uk/691 (accessed 15 January 2008).

Index

According to Queeney, 1, 7, 8, 11, 16, 17, 103, 134, 159–66
Ackroyd, Peter, 9, 17, 135, 160
Another Part of the Wood, 9, 10, 14, 19, 26, 27–36, 38, 46, 47, 50, 51, 53, 61, 64, 88, 106
Apollonian/Dionysian motif, 48, 92, 122
Aristotle, 14
Austen, Jane, 8
Awfully Big Adventure, An, 2, 7, 8, 9, 10, 14, 19, 102, 103, 125–32, 134, 154

Bainbridge, Beryl: childhood, family, and education, 1–6; critical reception, 6–7; influences, 4–5; marriage, children, and divorce, 2–3; nominations and prizes, 7; perspectives about the past, 1, 4–5, 16, 57, 74, 102–4
Baker, John F., 7
Barnes, Julian, 17, 135
Birthday Boys, The, 16, 17–18, 103, 134, 135–45, 152, 156
Bottle Factory Outing, The, 7, 9, 10, 14, 15, 26, 47, 48, 61–73, 77, 78, 79, 85, 86, 91, 94, 106, 112, 120, 122, 125, 144, 157
Bradbury, Malcolm, 8, 47
Byatt, A. S., 9, 17, 135

character types, 26, 50, 54, 77, 79, 85, 92, 106, 112
childhood and adolescence, depictions of, 24, 37–46, 51, 54–56, 86, 88–93, 102, 115, 127–32, 154, 160
Collected Stories, 4
comedy, 6, 9–15, 20, 28, 48, 58, 59, 61, 62, 67, 70, 71, 72, 73, 74, 81, 85, 86, 91, 96, 98, 100–101, 105, 109–10, 111, 112–13, 116–17, 131, 144–45, 146, 161

Dickens, Charles, 4, 11
Drabble, Margaret, 9, 17, 134

Dressmaker, The, 7, 9, 14, 19, 26, 27, 47, 48–61, 62, 63, 64, 68, 69, 71, 72, 75, 76, 85, 86, 91, 92, 112, 120, 125, 126, 127, 154, 157

English Journey, 1, 2, 3, 4, 5, 102, 125
Every Man for Himself, 7, 16, 134, 145–52

family relations, depictions of, 28, 30, 35, 39–40, 45–46, 53, 58–59, 60, 68, 78–79, 83, 86, 88–94, 106–7, 120, 126–28, 149, 153–54, 161
Filthy Lucre, 1, 5 10, 16, 125
Fleishman, Avrom, 16–17, 118
Forever England, 102–3, 135
Fowles, John, 17, 134
friendship, depictions of, 22, 26, 32, 38, 41, 44, 53, 63, 64, 130, 148, 163, 165
Front Row, 5

gender relations and feminism, 27, 30–31, 42–43, 47–48, 64, 66–67, 70, 72, 75, 77, 83–84, 85, 89, 91, 95, 99–100, 102, 106, 112, 121–24, 150, 154, 155, 161, 164–65

Harriet Said, 2, 9, 19, 36–46, 47, 48, 49, 50, 51, 64, 65, 86, 88, 106, 125, 163
Haycroft, Anna, 16
Head, Dominic, 9
Herbert, Christopher, 12
historical fiction, 8, 15–18, 118–19, 134–35, 145, 152–53, 159
Holmes, Frederick, 135
"How I Began," 4–5, 10–11
Hutcheon, Linda, 17, 119, 135, 153

Injury Time, 7, 9, 10, 13, 14, 20, 27, 74, 94–101, 102, 103, 110, 112, 118, 144, 145, 146

Kermode, Frank, 6, 76
Kronenberger, Louis, 10

Lawrence, D. H., 4
Liverpool as setting, 3, 51, 52, 84, 106–7, 125, 126, 154

Master Georgie, 7, 16, 17, 134, 152–59
misanthropic imaginary topography and pessimism, 6, 11, 14–15, 20, 26, 27, 29, 35–36, 37, 46, 47, 53, 61, 62, 74–75, 80, 85, 96, 101, 102, 111, 118, 125, 126, 132, 139, 152, 156, 165–66
miscommunication as motif, 20, 22, 25, 33–34, 65, 67, 70, 75, 91, 94, 96–98, 107, 114, 117, 121, 125, 131, 150, 152, 158, 161–62, 166
Mo, Timothy, 17
Mum and Mr. Armitage, 102

O'Neill, Patrick, 11, 12, 14, 20, 33, 48–49, 118

Phillips, Caryl, 17
postmodernism, 17, 134–36, 153
Punter, David, 20, 51, 73

Quiet Life, A, 9, 27, 74, 86–94

Rayner, Alice, 12–13, 14, 75
Rennison, Nick, 7–8, 9
Richetti, John, 19–20

Scanlan, Margaret, 17
social novel, 8–9, 19, 47
Something Happened Yesterday, 5
Stamirowska, Krystyna, 61, 72, 86
Steinbeck, John, 4
Sweet William, 9, 14, 15, 26, 27, 74, 75–86, 91, 94

violence as motif, 10–11, 48, 89, 91, 96, 98, 101, 107, 115, 120, 123–24, 131, 132, 158–59

Watson's Apology, 11, 16, 17, 102, 104, 118–24, 162
Weekend With Claude, A, 6, 8, 9, 11, 15, 19, 21–27, 28, 29, 38, 46, 47, 53, 61, 64, 75, 87, 94, 130, 150
Welch, Denton, 4
Wennö, Elisabeth, 7, 37
Williams, Nigel, 17
Winter Garden, 9, 10, 13, 14, 102, 110–18, 130, 144, 145, 146
Winterson, Jeanette, 17, 134

Young Adolf, 5, 9, 13, 16, 17, 102, 103–10, 118, 125, 130, 146, 154, 162